What Ever Happened to Mom's Apple Pie?

Books by John Keats

What Ever Happened to Mom's Apple Pie?

Of Time and an Island

Eminent Domain

You Might As Well Live

See Europe Next Time You Go There

The New Romans

The Sheepskin Psychosis

Howard Hughes

They Fought Alone

The Insolent Chariots

Schools Without Scholars

The Crack in the Picture Window

What Ever Happened to Mom's Apple Pie?

John Keats

Houghton Mifflin
Company Boston
1976

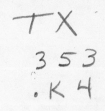
Library of Congress Cataloging in Publication Data

Keats, John, date
What ever happened to mom's apple pie?

1. Food.   2. Food industry and trade — United States.
3. Marketing (Home economics)   I. Title.
TX353.K4   641.3   75-44459
ISBN 0-395-24298-3

Printed in the United States of America

C 10 9 8 7 6 5 4 3 2 1

Eating and sleeping are a waste of time.

—*Gerald Ford, President of the United States*

A Table of Discontents

HORS D'OEUVRES

Introduction

Above the Fruited Plain — A Food Note to History, 1

SOUPS DU JOUR

Down on the Farm

Granny Rowed a Gravy Boat, 5
Goodbye, Mr. Bosch, 16
Monopoly's the Name of the Game, 22
Green Tomatoes and Dead Yellow Birds, 32

ENTRÉES

Hey, Diddle Diddle, the Men in the Middle

More Is Lost in the Process, 51
Argument on a Hilltop, 56
When the Price of Sugar Cubed, 62

Hamburger à la Broad, 69
Price and Paranoia, 74

SALADS

To Market, to Market, to Pay Through the Nose

Shopping with Kafka, 101
That's What's So Special About Them, 107
A Defensive Alternative, 127

NUTS

Please Pass the Guilt

The New Vegetarians, 135
The Ten-Foot Egg, 142

JUST DESSERTS

Eating Out for a Change

How Doggy Is Your Bag, Dad?, 157

DEMI TASSE

What's for Dinner Tonight?

Tales of Many Wives, 173

LIQUEURS

How to Survive in the Land of More

America: Take It or Leave It, 188
A Thought for Food, 215

Introduction

Above the Fruited Plain —
A Food Note to History

Once upon a time, what we ate determined the way we lived. This, in turn, had everything to do with what there was to eat where we lived. Before women invented agriculture, our antique longfathers chased down, killed, and ate whatever they could find running, hopping, or flying about the neighborhood, including strangers. They simultaneously tasted whatever grew there, no doubt spitting out most of it.

Now if, for one reason or another, a tribe found itself shut off upon a rocky seacoast that was otherwise devoid of terrestrial animal life and only sparsely covered with edible plants, the people turned, perforce, to the sea. From wading shore scavengers to fishermen to sailors to mercantile imperialists was only a matter of several tens of thousands of years of evolution, all of it sustained by a diet running strongly to seafood. The point is, what they ate first determined their employment, and next, their subsequent destiny.

Likewise, within the marches of the mainlands, the nature of the food supply was the determining factor. Nothing was more natural or inevitable than that nomads who followed animal herds across savannahs should eventually rise to the dignity of herdsmen; or that the eventual discovery of agriculture should give rise to the gardening of whatever grew in the area, and, from this meager start, to the creation of stable communities once gardening led to farming on a scale that produced a surplus of food beyond immediate need.

The development of a stable community based on agriculture was the prerequisite of civilization. The step from a village of gardeners to a more complex community could not, however, be taken until farming reached such a point of proficiency that it no longer required the full employment of all members of the community. When this point was reached, then what people ate became much less determinant of the way people lived. If not everyone was needed to work on the land, then those who were not so employed could do something else instead: the way was now open to long centuries of marvels and horrors.

Much has changed since the days of the first Middle Eastern city states, but in the centuries since then, and well into our own in America, all of the world's civilizations have been maintained by an agriculture that demanded the labor of a large majority. The relationship between food and the people who produced it and ate it has, until a very few years ago in our country, remained obvious and intimate. For example, in medieval Europe the typical peasants who fed the town lived with their animals within the walls at night, all of them walking to the adjacent fields in the safer light of dawn. Cultivation was parochial, understood by all. To know what there was to eat, one had only to climb the watchtower to see it growing or moving in the fields below. Such is still the case in Italian hill towns today.

But such is not the case in America. There are children among us, third-generation urban Americans, who have never seen food growing, and who would not recognize it as food if they did see it. A young visitor to our house was recently astonished to learn that potatoes could be mashed; she had heretofore thought that mashed potatoes came out of a box. Potatoes, yes; she had seen them before. But not mashed potatoes made from potatoes. As recently as two generations ago such a child would have been unimaginable.

To put the matter in more general terms, the relationship between Americans and food is no longer obvious or intimate. Only a small minority of our people work upon the land. Most of us are now strangers to it. Mechanical slaves till our fields, reap, pack, process, and deliver our bounty to our friendly computerized neighborhood supermarkets, and as a result of this progress, what we eat by no means determines the way we live. Instead, quite the reverse is true.

Nowadays in America, *how we live determines what we eat,* and this diametric reversal in the original order of things, seen most completely in our country within the last few decades, is beginning to be evident elsewhere in the world as well.

It is precisely because of the way we now live that some of the links in our food chain are weak, others are crooked, and a few are downright poisonous. Because of the way we live, it is increasingly difficult to go to the supermarket and emerge with fresh, tasty food that will be good for us to eat, purchased at a price we can afford. Whether this need be the case, or whether the situation will worsen, depends on our willingness to do something about it.

It is not enough simply to gripe about the food that is offered to us; to complain that it is too fattening, salty, sugary, stale, fake, unappetizing, deficient in nutrition — or to say that much of our food is expensive junk and that one Colonel McFinger's Howardburger Stand is just one too chicken-lickin' many of them. Valid though these complaints may be, they cannot merely be posted off to The Editor or the grand jury. All such complaints must be lodged against those who have conspired to create the modern American way of life. Then, only too often, it will be seen that the proper address is our own.

Not to put too fine a point upon it, if you and I and the folks next door wish to enjoy a more varied diet of better foods than we now consume, the remedy will involve our making substantial changes in the way we live.

In order to see what we are up against and how it came about, I propose that we go down the food chain link by link, from farm to table. After that, we can think about what might be done, or undone, in order that we may be able to eat well in a land that, for all that has been done to it, is still a land of plenty.

Down on the Farm

Granny Rowed a Gravy Boat

Close to dawn on any average day, you could look for Grandpa walking behind the mules while Granny slopped the hogs and scattered scraps to the chickens.

The time would be 1917, before we entered the First World War. It was a time when relatively few Americans lived in cities. Everyone else lived in small towns or villages or on the farm. In Grandpa's case, which was a fairly typical one, the farm was a little more than a hundred acres of gently rolling land. In addition to the mules, pigs, and chickens, there was a horse, a cow, a family of hounds, a vegetable garden, berry bushes, fruit trees, beehives, a corn field, a hay field, a woodlot, and a pond that Grandpa made by damming a stream that had brook trout in it.

I shall idyll you no idylls: Grandpa and Granny and everyone else in the family damned near broke their backs eighteen hours a day, six days a week, and often enough on those Sundays when the dam went out or when the hay had to be got in while the weather held or whenever any of a dozen other acts of God presented itself upon the Sabbath. Grandpa and Granny liked living in the country and they liked farming well enough, but it would be stretching a point to say they were tied to their ancestral acres by bonds of love. Rather, they were stuck there right up to their red necks, and though they did not leave the farm voluntarily, they were by no means sorry to move to the city. Grandpa would sooner have raised money than food any day of the week. Of course they enjoyed their homemade sausage. But if they had had the choice between killing and dressing out their hogs and buying a plastic package of weiners, Grandpa and Granny would have snapped up today's pink-colored fastfood grease-tubes faster than you can say "Hot dog!" And, rather than hang a ham for months from the chimney flitch, they would have gladly settled for one of today's Chicago waterwings that have been injected with a fluid vaguely flavored like smoke, and that have all the full-bodied texture of double-folded Kleenex.

In saying these things, I mean no disrespect for the honored gaffer and his kindly crone. I am merely concerned for facts, and the fact is that America's old folks were just as potentially lazy as we are. Although they raised, sold, and ate good food, it was curiously true that they did not give food the first priority in their scheme of values. Perhaps if familiarity did not breed contempt, abundance enabled them to take food for granted while they fixed their sights on targets more important to them. But they certainly did eat hugely and well.

Specifically, *like other ordinary Americans of their time*, Grandpa and Granny dined on oysters, Maryland terrapin, lobsters, planked shad, bass, and trout. They ate succulent squabs, roast wild pigeons, ducks, geese, and many other game birds, as well as a range of domestic fowl, including the guinea hens that Grandpa shot off the barn roof. They consumed venison, hares, squirrels, porterhouse steak stuffed with olives, and all manner of chops, steaks, joints, and roasts derived from sheep, cattle, and swine. They sat down to daily four-course dinners that were concluded with plump round cakes and pies made at home that day, and washed all this down with coffee, freshly roasted and ground at home, if not also with hock and claret. Nor was this daily repast their only ration. There would have been porridge, ham steaks, eggs, potatoes, biscuits and red gravy, biscuits and honey, and coffee for breakfast. Soup, meat, bread, fruit, and cheese were in the worker's lunch pail.

Evidence that such an opulent diet was *not* the privilege of an elite, but was common fare, may be had from almost anyone whose memory goes back to the First World War, or, if you distrust the over-roseate recollections of the aged, you can read about it for yourself in a book written by Marion Harris Neil and published in 1917 by Proctor and Gamble, the manufacturers of Crisco. The book, *A Calendar of Dinners*, suggested 365 menus to the general public, beginning with Miss Neil's idea of what to serve on New Year's Day: a black bean soup, roast leg of mutton with currant jelly, stewed tomatoes, baked sweet potatoes, Macédoine salad, cheese straws, fruit cake, and coffee.

That this was not a holiday meal may be seen by Miss Neil's menu for the following day: Palestine soup, jugged hares, Brussels sprouts, potato puffs, endive salad, cheese fingers, vanilla soufflé, and coffee.

So it went throughout Miss Neil's year. For 365 days she would have the joyous American housewife blithely turning out dinners consisting of at least eight different foods, even in high summer. A typical July menu called for clam bisque, lamb chops, escalloped corn, creamed sweet potatoes, German salad, cheese drops, strawberry Bavarian cream, and coffee. Never once did she mention leftovers, possibly because there would have been little left over in an age when people said waste not, want not, and when children were enjoined to eat everything on their plates. Every dinner began with a soup, and although canned goods were plentifully available, Miss Neil did not necessarily envision a housewife opening a can to warm a soup. Nor did she once mention bread. The presence of home-baked bread on the table could be assumed, like the presence of plates.

The purpose of the book was to sell Crisco to a mass market and thereby make both Proctor and Gamble rich. The menus therefore included at least one dish per dinner that could be prepared with Crisco. But the impressive fact is that the book would have had no meaning to the general public, at which it was aimed, if it had not been the custom of most Americans to sit down to a daily four-course feast; if the good things the book recommends had not been readily available at prices the public could easily afford; if there had not been sufficient space, time, and womanpower available in the American home to prepare, serve, and consume a banquet as a matter of daily routine.

As one turns the pages of Miss Neil's year, it is immediately apparent that virtually all of the fruits and vegetables she suggests would have been in season. Since there was no trucking industry then, no flash-freezing, no home freezers, no giant food-processing industry, and no multibillion-dollar chains of national supermarkets, it follows that the produce must have been locally available. Whenever the menus called for something not in season, such as stewed tomatoes in January, the requirement was for something that could have been, and most probably was, preserved by home canning. The inclusion of oysters, lobsters, Maryland terrapin, and shad in Miss Neil's book indicates that Crisco's primary market was America's populous East Coast. The demographic center of the nation had not yet moved to Kansas. East Coast seafood would, however, have been available in Chicago, for special express trains of refrigerator cars took it there before an express passenger service was established. The presence of all manner of game and fresh produce in Miss Neil's menus otherwise reminds us that the East Coast was not then a smear of poisonous cities very nearly contiguous. Like the rest of the nation, it was predominantly open country, checkered with single-family farms like Grandpa's.

In 1917, less than a lifetime ago, Americans still lived in a way that was characteristic of societies since the dawn of civilization: the production of food required the efforts of a majority of the population; land was a primary source of wealth as well as the only source of food; the cities were small and drew upon the immediate hinterland for the bulk of their foodstuffs; the relationship of people and food was intimate and obvious. True, Henry Ford had been stamping out Model T's for nine years, like a madwoman with a cookie cutter, and America was caught up in the excitement of becoming the world's principal industrial power as she produced armaments for the Allies and herself. Women were beginning to work in offices and young men were moving from the country to jobs in the burgeoning industries, but in its major respects America was still a horsecollar civilization. There were one hundred fifty million fewer of us then, and whether we lived on the farm or in a village or a town, most of us lived in houses large enough to accommodate three generations of a family. The typical American house stood on grounds ample enough to permit its residents to grow a considerable supply of fruits and vegetables in the back garden, and this was true of many city dwellings as well.

For most of us, then, the familiar things would include the

pond ice stored in the icehouse under sawdust, the foot-thick collar of cream on the milk cans, the coffee-grinder in the kitchen, the women's hands white with flour, the wood stove and the great stack of stove wood in the shed outside the kitchen door. Most particularly, the images are of the many people who lived in the house. In those days nearly everyone believed woman's place was in the home, and there were apt to be several at home to help with what nearly everyone believed to be women's work. Also present, in their roles as food-providers, wood-choppers, and eaters, were men: one old man, at least one younger one, and, it was hoped, two or three head of boys. Whatever the work, almost everyone walked to it.

The overall impression is of a relatively simple society that had much to do with its hands — and one that had a great deal to eat, and ate quite a lot because it needed the fuel. Everyone then took more exercise, in the course of an ordinary day, than Americans do now. This was not only because they lived in a larger space, but also because more was required of a man who cranked his Ford or harnessed his horse to drive to town than is required of a man who now turns an ignition switch and sits in a four-wheeled sofa that takes him there. The woman whose cake-making began with a visit to the henhouse and who had to beat the batter with a spoon was involved in more activity than the one who now opens a box and uses an electric beater. Children were much more active than they are today: there was more space available for their play inside and outside the house, even in the cities. And in the cities the children would walk to and from school twice a day inasmuch as they all walked home at midday for lunch. The greater expense of physical energy to perform almost every task doubtless had some-thing, if not everything, to do with the amount of food everyone consumed, and obesity was not then an American problem, nor was malnutrition — as is now the case.

Between then and now our standards of physical and mental health steadily deteriorated. Military statistics, precisely applicable to the period we are discussing, confirm this. They show that, ever since World War I, the Army has progressively lowered its physical and mental requirements for admission, not because it wanted to, but because it had to if it was to obtain a sufficient number of conscripts. Despite this steady reduction in standards, the percentage of those rejected for service relentlessly increased. The statistics say that the young American soldier of 1917 was far tougher and healthier, and had fewer personality defects and mental imbalances, than his son who went to World War II, and that he was in these respects infinitely the superior of his taller but weaker grandson who went to Vietnam. If an older man should complain that they're not making boys like they used to, he is not necessarily mooning about some imaginary good old days when men were men. It is more likely that he is stating a simple fact.

Seventy-five percent of American youth now have acute atherosclerosis by the time they are twenty. Atherosclerotic cardiovascular disease is by far the leading cause of death in the United States, and most of the causes of this disease — including hypertension, excessive blood cholesterol, and obesity — are directly related to nutrition.

Speaking to the last factor, Dr. Jean Mayer, a Harvard professor of nutrition, has said he thinks America's obesity "is largely a result of lack of exercise. Actually, our data show that Americans eat less now than they did in 1900. But they exercise so much less that they eat more than they ought to, and as a result are overweight." *

Another reason for the outrageously high incidence of

---

* Dr. Mayer's quotations are derived from his article in the October 1974 edition of *Physician's World.*

atherosclerosis in America is the fact that so much of our diet consists of foods that directly contribute to hypertension and excessive blood cholesterol. Referring to the incidence of this disease among the young, Dr. Mayer said, "That should cause a complete re-evaluation of the way we rear our children, especially the way in which we feed them."

So it might. And so should the evidence coming in from the United States Department of Agriculture, which shows that Americans are becoming progressively undernourished, as well as badly nourished, in these years of what we call plenty. Agriculture Department dietary surveys show that a smaller fraction of Americans received adequate amounts of nutrients in 1965 than in 1955, and the prediction is for a further skid when the 1975 figures are in. Unbelievable as it may seem, some Americans are now starving to death even as they gain weight. The reason is that the food they eat does not nourish them.

Given as we all are to worshipping science and to imagining American progress as a steadily rising line on a graph, it may come as something of a nasty surprise to be forced to admit that the Americans of 1917 were better fed, in every possible meaning of the term, than Americans are today. They had a much greater variety of foodstuffs available to them; their food was fresher and more nutritious; it tasted better for being fresh. The 1917 Americans not only ate more food than we now do, but, with all due allowance made for the difference in buying power between the 1917 and 1975 dollars, they paid less money for food than we do.

The reasons why we now pay more for less and worse are bound up in the changes that have taken place in America during the past fifty-eight years. In this incredibly short time America has experienced four major wars, a convulsive economic depression, a material prosperity unique in human history, a population explosion, the creation of an industrial technology that proliferated exponentially, and the simultaneous development of something absolutely revolutionary: an agricultural system based upon the employment of a small and ever diminishing minority of the populace. In less than six decades we moved from relative bucolic isolation into a world of multinational conglomerates; from a direct observation of barnyard amours to a teleview of machines copulating in outer space. Both as a consequence of these changes and in order to bring many of them about, we altered drastically the pattern of our lives.

No longer do three generations of an American family live cooperatively on the farm or in the big houses of the nation's small town Elm Streets. Most of us have left the country for the noxious sprawls that are better known not as cities but as metropolitan areas. Grandpa and Granny have disappeared, and so have the uncles and the cousins and the aunts. Nowadays the family has been reduced to Mom, Pop, and the kids, inhabiting an urban cubicle like cliff swallows in a hole. It is by no means the rule that this minimal family eats breakfast, or any other meal, together.

If primary responsibility for getting food on the table still belongs to the American mother, and if she is also going to be stuck alone with all of life's domestic fatigue details, which were once shared among herself, Granny, Aunt Dot, and Sister Sue, she is most unlikely to have the time, energy, or inclination to open the first hour of her long day by leaping athletically out of bed to begin the preparation of the three-course, eight-food breakfast of 1917, even assuming that anyone these days would want such a meal or had time to eat it.

Instead, she is much more likely to open a jar to make instant coffee; to open a can of concentrate to make a shaker full of something she is willing to accept as a reasonable substitute for fresh orange juice, to put a box of dry cereal on the kitchen table — and say the hell with it. Pop and the kids can find their own glasses, cups, spoons, and bowls when each arrives in the kitchen at his different time.

Then, since Pop goes one way to his work and the kids go off in another way to school and since Mom quite possibly fares forth in a third direction to a job of her own, no lunch is prepared in this, our happy home.

The family's one opportunity to enjoy a decent meal comes in the evening when the minimal family reassembles. The likelihood that this will be a four-course, eight-food affair is quite remote. Once again, for reasons involving a lack of time, energy, inclination, and sometimes money, the evening meal is apt to consist of one course of three foods that can be prepared as quickly as possible and that cost a minimum of thought, time, and money to buy. It is often the case, particularly in the commuting suburbs, that Mom and Pop will share this feast alone. Pop comes home late, and the children will have eaten earlier, dining on something else, such as TV dinners, which they pick at while numbly sitting in a mindless trance before the tiny screen. If, by day's end, no one in this family has much appetite, the reason for it could be that all of them had been nibbling junk throughout the day.

Writing in the *New York Times Magazine*,* John L. Hess reports that "Dr. Paul A. Fine, a psychological consultant to the food industry, has found that *the typical American seldom sits down to a proper family meal;* instead, he or she has an average of twenty 'food contacts' a day, feeding on 'Oreos, peanut butter, Crisco, TV dinners, cake mix, macaroni and cheese, Pepsi and Coke, pizzas, Jell-O, hamburgers, Rice-a-Roni, Spaghetti-Os, pork and beans, Heinz catsup, and instant coffee.' "

* The August 18, 1974, issue. Italics added.

It is sobering to reflect that such a diet might be a matter
of *choice;* to think that today's ordinary American might
actually prefer twenty daily contacts with junk to the daily
feasts of fresh foods his grandparents enjoyed. And there is
even evidence to suggest that such might be the case. For
Mr. Hess also reports that "food industry chemists told the
newspaper that the public now rejected real orange or
pineapple juice or real coffee as tasting strange; a brand of
catsup developed to preserve a fresh tomato flavor was a
failure until the sauce was scorched and a metallic tinge
added to make it taste familiar." *

It is also sobering to reflect that the typical Americans to
whom Mr. Hess's article referred include in their number
various scientists who work at Philadelphia's Eastern Regional Research Center, a laboratory of the United States
Department of Agriculture. One of them, who should and
did know better, admitted he ate junk food in the laboratory's cafeteria, "like a cheeseburger and a Coke, just something to put in my stomach to help me get through the rest of
the day." Horrified by himself, he took to watching the
similar habits of his learned colleagues and to timing them.
He discovered the average noon feeder spent a total of
twenty minutes in the cafeteria: ten minutes standing in line
and the other ten eating at a plastic table. He agreed that we
eat what we do because of the way we live, and that, if we
lived differently, we could eat differently. Recently returned
from Rome, where he had attended a scientific convention
dealing with the world's food problems, he spoke longingly
of the good food and fresh fruits of Italy, of the time Italians
spent at table, and of what seemed to him to be the slower
pace of Italian life. But, he said, since we live the way we do
and since this implies our spending ten minutes at noon to

---

* Ibid.

lunch on junk, government research was taking the form of finding ways to fortify the junk.

"If that's what we eat, we might as well make it nourishing," he said pragmatically, and talked of plans to add iron to breakfast cereals and whey to Coke. The way matters stood now, he said, the box was more nutritious than the cereal it contained.

He said this with a mordant smile, as if it were an office joke, but he may have had in mind a British dietary laboratory experiment that made precisely this point. Rats fed on shredded cereal boxes received more nourishment than rats fed on the contents of those boxes: sugar and milk were present in identical quantities in each case. While we think about this, we might also reflect that the box costs more than the cereal.

We shall presently have much, much more to say about junk food, convenience food, and wholly synthetic foods, and about the advertisers who look upon all this swill and find it good, and hire little children to appear on television to lie and coax and whine for more. But now I should like to return to the farm.

Goodbye, Mr. Bosch

Today there is a traffic light at about where Grandpa's pigpen used to be — it starts and stops the flow in and out of a shopping center — and close to any average dawn the only thing you're liable to find moving thereabouts would be a police car with its radio squawking. I have said that American cities once drew their food supplies largely from the immediate hinterland, but this is no longer the case: 70 percent of our lettuce, 76 percent of our cauliflower, and more than half of our potatoes, tomatoes, and celery come from California, no matter where you buy them.

Grandpa's farm and all the farms that used to march around it have become an urban sprawl of filling stations, shopping centers, and a regimented expanse of look-alike, built-alike suburban houses, spilling out into a county that once provided Philadelphia, Pennsylvania, with food that was good to eat.

Farther out, past this smear, what is left of the county is, or still could be, prime farmland. But only two single-family general farms remain in operation there today. The families who live on them have been there for two hundred years without ever becoming rich, and the current generations narrowly survive on the basis of their roadside sale of produce to the tourists who pour out of the city on weekends to enjoy what has become a tourist county full of artsy-craftsy shops that sell ready-made Early American antiques. The two farmers also have a custom trade among the wealthy exurbanites who have settled in the old stone houses in and around what has become an artsy-craftsy village that is otherwise regarded as a good commute. By this, the exurbanites mean that it does not take them quite two hours to proceed by automobile and train from their quasi-Early American splendor to the quite genuine money-making squalor of New York City. Most of the farms remaining in what is left of the county produce nothing. They are the residences of wealthy commuters, operated as tax losses, decorated by a scattering of Black Angus in the middle distances beyond the swimming pools and the tennis courts. The other farms are of two kinds, the first of which is not a farm at all. One has a waterwheel, made in 1672, that still turns and presses apples into cider. Its owner, a lineal descendant and namesake of the Hiram Bosch who made the waterwheel, was once a farmer like all his fathers before him.

"But in the thirties," he said, "farm labor was twenty cents an hour for a slow worker, and thirty cents for a good one. Then the New Deal came in and people started leaving the country for the city to go on relief, because you could get fifty cents an hour for doing next to nothing on the WPA."

At this time the county population began to undergo a curious change. As country people moved to the city to make money by going on relief, New York City people began to move to the country to save money by living a simpler life — telling each other they would never starve if they had land on which to raise their own food. Not that they ever did this, of course; it was just their fond belief that, if things got truly bad, they could always turn to farming. In any case, city people began to buy up then-cheap county land, and thus was exurbia born. Farmer Bosch, meanwhile, was lucky to be able to find enough country people still living in the area who were willing to help him tend his orchards and farmland at a price he was able to pay. Thus, during the Depression, he continued to truck apples and produce to Philadelphia's Dock Street, where a commission agent would sell the bulk of it for him. The rest of his truckload was spoken for.

"I used to make deliveries," he said, "to Kugler's and Stouffer's restaurants, to the Germantown Hospital and the Lankenau Hospital kitchens, and to neighborhood grocers who would want different things for different customers. I used to grow Cortlands, Turleys, Rome Beauties, McIntoshes, and Winesaps. Different grocers would want different kinds. I had four thousand birds, and I could deliver live or fresh-killed chickens and farm-fresh eggs.

"But now," he said, "farm workers, good or bad, get three and a half dollars an hour, and even at that they are hard to find. And there isn't any Dock Street anymore. Now they have a computerized and automated Food Distribution Center in Philadelphia, and nobody there wants small lots of different sizes and grades of different apples. There aren't any corner groceries anymore. There are supermarkets. They won't talk to you unless you have a trailer load of Red

Delicious, size eighty or seventy-two. That means eighty to a box, or seventy-two.

"All that," Farmer Bosch said, referring to the Distribution Center and the supermarkets, "came in after the war. The hospitals and the restaurants stopped buying my apples because they couldn't afford to pay people to peel them. They buy peeled apples from an apple-peeling concern that peels them by the ton and soaks them in ascorbic acid to preserve a fresh appearance. No, of course they're not as good as fresh-peeled apples. But when a restaurant or a hospital wants to make applesauce, I suppose the freshness doesn't matter to them so much as the cost does, and when they need fifty pounds of peeled apples for the recipe, they can buy exactly fifty pounds of peeled apples instead of trying to guess at the weight of the peelings, and the cost of the service is less than the cost of labor, because the apples are peeled by machine."

Mr. Bosch did not want to sell his farm, even though any of a score of exurban millionaires would have been glad to bid for it. The money would have been less valuable to him than the sentimental value of remaining upon the Crown Grant that had been his family's possession for three hundred years. What he wanted to be, and once was but can no longer be, was an American yeoman, living and working on his own freehold, beholden to no one. But in order to remain on his land he had to become a businessman.

"If you like old Colonial farms and good old-fashioned cider," his leaflet says, "come out and pay us a call when you come out to see the Fall colors. We've been here since Hiram Bosch built the waterwheel in 1672, and the wheel is still turning and pressing our apples. We grow our own fine apples and make our cider the old-fashioned way with nothing added. No preservatives, no pasteurizing, just good apples. We also have hand-eating apples, and apples for baking, for pies, for coddling, for applesauce, for strudel, for Brown Betty, for green apple tarts — just the right apple for whatever you like. We have eggs, chickens, and capons too — we select our poultry each week at its prime, and quick-freeze it in our freezers."

Mr. Bosch has paid a price for this advertisement, because he has always been an honest man and the advertisement is something more and less than the truth. In fact, the farm does not grow the apples it presses or sells. The Bosch orchards are untended ghosts. Nor does the farm produce one chicken or one egg. The apples are bought from other people's orchards, and the birds are raised, killed, and frozen in a sixty thousand-bird factory operated by a company several miles away. The Bosch farm is, in fact, a retail store that, like any other, buys at wholesale and marks up its wares — in this case, fobbing them off as its own. The cider is good, however, and the apples do at least come from Pennsylvania, which is more than can be said for some of the country farms that sell apples brought to them by transcontinental truck-trailers.

The orchards from which Mr. Bosch buys his apples exemplify the other kind of farm still found in the county. It is the kind of farm that practices what the Agriculture Department calls monoculture, the production of only one crop. If a farmer grows apples, he grows only apples; if tomatoes, then only tomatoes; if he is a dairy farmer, he does not also grow beans or even hay. One of the orchards supplying apples to Mr. Bosch belongs to Maynard Grayson, who has managed to stay solvent in America by becoming small.

"Farming," Mr. Grayson said, "is a lot of hard work and it's all a gamble on the weather, and while you're working and gambling, your fixed costs keep going up. The bigger you are, the more you have to go to machines that take the

place of hand labor, and the machines get more complicated
and expensive every year. If you have machines, then you
have to have a repair shop, and next thing you know, you are
hiring mechanics. Your fuel costs more, and so does your
power, your fertilizer, your sprays, your implements, your
tools. The bigger you are, the more you'll have to go hiring
office clerks, and you'll be paying union wages for truck
hauling, and the bigger you are, the faster you can go broke.
Drought or hail can ruin you on a larger scale. So then you
have to go to the bank to hire more money, and it keeps
costing more to hire money and the money doesn't buy as
much as it did the day you hired it.

"You can't sell loose apples in crates or baskets if you're
big. Even here, people come to buy apples, they don't want a
basket, they want five pounds, ten pounds, in a bag, and the
price of paper bags is going up. Anyway, when you're big,
you need plastic bags, which cost more than paper ones, and
you have to hire labor or buy machines to bag your apples,
and the plastic bags need labels and seals, and the plastic
bags go into special boxes for shipment — and all this
labeling and sealing and plastic and special boxes isn't really
wanted or asked for by the customer who only wants to be
able to buy five pounds of apples at the store, and none of it
adds a damned thing to the taste or quality of those apples.
There just gets to be so much you can't eat that gets into
apples nowadays. Nobody eats clerks or plastic bags, but
there they are, right in the price you pay. I never want to get
big, like those growers out in the state of Washington. They
grow for handling and preservation, not for variety or taste.
They say their apples just have to be good enough to get by.
Just get by, just get by, that's all they say. So they all grow
Red Delicious, which is a dumb kind of apple to eat unless
you pick it off a tree and eat it, but they shine up pretty,
which is why they grow them, I guess, and now I hear the big

growers are going to wax their apples for a longer shelf-life, and why anyone wants to add wax to a Red Delicious, I don't know — the peels have plenty of wax in them as it is; it's what makes them shine when you polish them. What all this wax will do to the consumer, I don't know either, but I do know he'll be buying a lot of wax along with all of the rest of the things he can't eat when he buys those apples. But that's what happens. If you're big, you wind up charging more for your product than the little independent farmer would, because of all you've had to add to it, and there isn't a thing you've put in it that makes your apples any better, but you have to charge the customer for it, anyway. I'd rather stay small."

Monopoly's the Name of the Game

The hinterland that fed the cities fifty-eight years ago is no longer capable of doing so, and not simply because so much of the land has been converted into a suburban smear. To be sure, that is one reason, but it is bound up in others that all have to do with the proliferation of the technological society that replaced the horsecollar one. And what happened to farmers in the counties around the eastern cities has, during the same years, happened to farmers elsewhere across the nation. In the past thirty years, the number of American farms has been reduced by half. The process is continuing.

Meanwhile, as the number of farmers and farms diminishes, America's annual tonnage of food produced keeps rising — and the variety and quality of that food keeps falling. Fewer and fewer produce more and more that is worth less and less at the farm gate, while the price goes up and up at the checkout counter. It is truly a miracle of our time.

It is also a peculiarly American miracle, proceeding from our historic belief that freedom of opportunity is a God-given right and that it implies a man's freedom to do unto others whatever the law allows him to do unto them. As applied to economics, this moral philosophy is called the free-enterprise system. The cardinal law of this system states that those with the most money are the most free to engage in the most enterprises. A parlor game called Monopoly, which American children learn as soon as they can count, perfectly illustrates how the system works. The rich become richer; the poor, poorer; and ultimately one player winds up owning everything. This, in rough measure, is what has been happening in business and industry in the past few decades of multinational corporate conglomerates, and it has been happening down on the farm as well. Briefly put, Americans have been leaving the land for the past fifty-eight years not so much because they have wanted to, as because they have been driven from it.

Some Americans began to leave the country for the city before the First World War, lured by the promise of more excitement than country life afforded, and by the promise of considerably more money for shorter hours of less arduous work. But this trickle of migrants to the city later swelled to a flood because of pressures brought about by technical advances and economic forces. The invention of tracked vehicles, reapers and binders, before the First World War, pointed the way. Once it was demonstrated that a man on a machine could plow more land more quickly and cheaply than he could by walking behind a mule, trying to guide it while wrestling with the plow and cursing every stone in the field, the days of horsecollar labor in America were plainly numbered. But before the advent of the one-man tractor, there appeared horse-drawn sowers, reapers, and binders, which soon became huge steam-powered reapers and binders (some of these still horse-drawn). In western grain lands, steam threshers, owned by entrepreneurs employing work gangs, contracted with farmers to glean the fields and separate the grain from the chaff, and the dawn of farming on a gigantic, corporate scale was at hand. The machines multiplied, became ever more sophisticated, and, as they became more sophisticated, the number of men required to tend them diminished. When the machines began to move themselves, there was no longer a need for so many horses and mules, and as the number of farm animals decreased there was a consequent decrease in the amount of manure that could be used as fertilizer. The day of synthetic fertilizer, therefore, began to dawn as well. The appearance of the machine on the farm presaged an agricultural revolution, and in consequence a revolutionary change in the entire American way of life, but it is more than doubtful if anyone was aware of this at the time. More than likely, the farmers and the manufacturers of the machines saw nothing but more money and better times ahead, and no one else saw anything ominous in the fact that, as farms were becoming larger and the number of animals was becoming smaller, the number of farm families and farm workers leaving the land for the cities was becoming something more than a trickle. It was becoming a spate.

Then came the Great Depression. Land and crop mortgages came due, and if the farmers were unable to meet their debts, the mortgages were foreclosed. The single-family general farm, with its characteristic hundred acres and its always precarious financial structure, was particularly vulnerable to a prolonged economic depression. The price the farmer receives for his produce has never been high in America, and during the Depression he received even less. With farm prices as low as they were, it became increasingly clear that the only economically viable farm was going to be a very large one, devoted to a single crop grown at the lowest possible cost. Low as Depression wages for farm hands might be, the cost of machine labor was lower still, and farm laborers were, as they put it, "tractored off the land." The spate of migrants to the cities now began to become a stream.

In this mean time, farmers were bringing a glut of food to market, thereby lowering its price to their further disadvantage. President Franklin D. Roosevelt's New Deal administration was full of notions for helping the farmer. The government would subsidize the farmers by giving them the difference between what their crops were actually worth on the current market and a price that would allow them to meet their expenses. The government would buy up surplus crops and store them at the taxpayers' expense. The government would pay farmers not to grow food and not to raise livestock. At the same time, the government would help the farmers lower their costs by bringing cheap electric power to the farms — an improvement that had the somewhat dubious effect of increasing the farmers' means of production while reducing their need for farm labor.

The number of large farms now grew. They were created by the consolidation of many contiguous small failed ones, and the purchasers included corporations such as life insurance companies — corporations that hired part-time employees to man the machines the corporation could afford to buy and that were essential to farming on the largest possible scale at the lowest possible cost. Enter now the "suitcase farmers" — the corporate employees who would arrive with suitcases in small Midland towns, rent rooms, and drive out to the grain fields each day to drive the machines that plowed and dressed the land, leaving when this was done and returning at a later season to operate the machines that brought in the harvest.

Agricultural production rose during the Depression. The

government bought the surplus, and the result was that Americans were then paying for food they did not eat, as well as paying to store it, as well as paying for food that they did eat, as well as paying for food that was neither stored nor eaten because it was not grown, and paying for livestock that was not raised, as well as paying for the social services that had to be created to minister to the needs of displaced field hands, who, without any suitcases, were arriving in growing numbers in the city slums. And this is still the case today. Before we believe the Agriculture Department's claim that we Americans pay less for our food than the citizens of any other Western nation, we should reckon in all the prices we *really* pay for it, including the price we are still paying for the social disruption that has ensued in the course of our conversion from a rural nation into an urban nation in less than a man's lifetime.

By the end of the Second World War, the American agricultural revolution was to all intents and purposes complete. The war had demanded that America produce unheard-of amounts of fighting men, arms, and food — all at once. Since millions of people were required to produce the arms, and thirteen million more of us marched off to use them, the process of consolidation and mechanization of farms was remarkably increased during the war in order to produce the food. One result of this was that the farm hands who had been soldiers discovered, on their return, that they had been tractored off the land while they had been away.

In the immediate postwar years, the migration to the cities became a flood. Up to the moment of our entrance in the war, a majority of Americans had lived in rural areas, and after the war a majority lived in metropolitan ones, and as it moved toward the cities, this majority increased like lemmings. The countryside became progressively less populous. Many a village became a ghost town as its storekeepers shut up shop for want of customers and moved to the cities, too.

It was during the first two postwar decades, while we silted up in cities, that Americans became the massive consumers of the mass-produced. We then entered upon what a friend calls the Age of the Slob. Behind his unkind remark lay his true meaning: as we lost a living space we had once enjoyed and a family life we had hitherto known, and as we exchanged independent work for fractional jobs, clean air for foul, and silence for noise, we tended to lose a sense of purpose and identity, and to become the inmates of a prison governed by an intolerable and inescapable version of Gresham's Law. This version said that not only does bad money drive good money out of the money market, but also that the shoddy drives out the good from every kind of mass market, including the markets for consumer goods, housing, education, and employment.

There is some force to this observation. For example, there was a time when a man's work said who he was. The names Smith, Baker, Cook, Fletcher, Wainwright, and a hundred others are testimony to this fact. As recently as the first decade of our century, the work a man did in America was apt to be the most important thing about him: it was the source of his pride and sense of place. But no more. Most of us now live in a kind of egalitarian middlemass anthill, geared to mass production and mass consumption; we are all bound up in a technological society dependent for its existence upon centralization, standardization, and the division of labor into fractions of tasks. In such a society, people are replaceable parts, and there is little about a fractional job in which any replaceable part can take the slightest satisfaction, much less find a sense of pride or place. In this situation, the replaceable part is interested more in how much money his job pays than in the job he does, and because his work cannot define him, he tends to state who he thinks he is, or who he thinks he ought to be, by how much money he makes and by what he buys with his money. Unfortunately, there is little of value for him to buy, read, see, or learn in a mass society, because such a society is predicated upon a constant search for the lowest common denominators. That which is offered for sale is that which can most commonly be sold, and this, according to my friend's version of Gresham, implies the production of the most junk to sell to the most slobs.

If urban American life resembles that of a corporate anthill, it should not be surprising to find it fed by corporate ants. This is indeed the case. The people who now give us each day our daily bread are the same wonderful folks who have given us the International Telephone and Telegraph Company. ITT and many other giant corporations are now calling the tune down on the farm. They have brought to agriculture the same methods of centralization and standard-ization that they otherwise apply to business and industry, and if the result is Slob Food, there should be nothing surprising about that.

There are those who regard the intrusion of big business into farming as an evil perpetrated with malice aforethought, but it is more realistic to regard it simply as an inevitable extension of the American genius for organization and of our national penchant for playing Monopoly. A large corpora-tion is no more evil than Farmer Brown. There never has been a farmer who wished he had less money and less land. During the Depression and after the war, large farmers gobbled up their less fortunate small neighbors, and the large farmers were in turn devoured by huge ones. Farmers are as fond of playing Monopoly as anyone else.

Corporations began to snap up huge farms during the Depression, and after the war the process accelerated in the years of corporate mergers. The mergers were designed to achieve what the financial Johnnies call diversification. This means putting your eggs into several baskets so as not to lose all of them if one of the baskets drops, and it also means increasing your opportunity to make even more money by having several different baskets of different eggs to sell. To diversify is to play real-life Monopoly; to see how it goes, let us pretend you are Johnson Johnson, president of Pan World Oil, Inc. You have more money than you will ever need for any combination of purposes whatsoever, JJ, but driven by your natural-born, red-blooded American competitive desire to acquire more and more of whatever it is, you begin to buy up other businesses in order to make even more money.

For example, you hear that Crankshaft Tractors is doing a dandy business making and selling tractors. A study indicates that if you put some Pan World Oil money into expanding Crankshaft's operations, then Crankshaft could make more tractors and more money. You press a buzzer and order an aide to buy Crankshaft Tractors, lock, stock, barrel, and goodwill. Pan World Oil is now in the tractor business: you have begun to diversify. You think about this for a moment, then thoughtfully purchase an iron mine and a steel company. It has occurred to you that your mine can sell its ore to your steel company, which can sell its steel to your tractor company, which will make the tractors that use your oil. You can easily arrange this series of sales, cheaply to your own companies but still making a profit at each step, meanwhile also selling your ore, your steel, and your tractors expensively to everyone else.

But hold! To think of tractors is to think of farms. Tractors spread fertilizer on farms. To think of fertilizers is also to think of pesticides, for some types of each are derived from petroleum bases. Why not buy up the fertilizer and pesticide companies that are now buying their oil from you? Once you have embarked on this perfectly logical line of thought, it is inevitable that you will think of buying the farm as well. You are now doing more than simply diversifying Pan World's interests. You are beginning to create what is called vertical integration, which is a very big thing in big business. You pause to think. From mine to foundry to tractors that use your oil to spread your fertilizer and spray your pesticide upon your farm to . . . to what?

Oh, yes! Now you have it! Farms raise food! Food is packaged and trucked to market. Wherefore you buy a package-making company, a trucking business, a wholesale produce marketing firm to act as your own middleman, a bank specializing in farm loans so that you can lend money to yourself at a favorable rate, and a nationwide chain of supermarkets. You are now in a position, JJ, to turn a dollar on every transaction that takes place all the way from a hole in the ground to some lucky family's dining ell, and every time you pass Go you can collect another billion dollars from the government in the form of crop subsidies.

You can do this, JJ, if Tenneco can. And who, or what, pray tell, is Tenneco? It might sound like something you rub on your spots, but it happens to be a real-life conglomerate engaged in the oil refinery business, the oil pipeline business, the chemical business, the shipbuilding, packaging, and retail sales businesses. In his book *The American Food Scandal*,* William Robbins tells the story of Tenneco's operations. According to Mr. Robbins, when Tenneco decided to go into farming, it had lots of Monopoly money to play with. The company had $4 billion stuffed away in its corporate mattress, and every fiscal year, when it passed Go, Tenneco collected $139 million. So, when it came to buying land, Tenneco did not stint. The corporation bought up one million four hundred thousand acres of Oregon, California,

* William Morrow and Company, Inc., New York, 1974.

New Mexico, and Arizona. With its purchase, Tenneco acquired a company that made tractors and farm machinery, and having bought all this, Tenneco then acquired its own middleman — the world's largest produce marketing company.

Agriculture was not the company's original interest, but once engaged upon it, Tenneco's directors gave the matter careful thought.

"Our goal in agriculture," their annual report said in 1970, "is integration from the seedling to the supermarket."

A diversified company with its hands on every link of the food chain can, at every link, turn a profit while selling to itself and even more of a profit by selling to others, particularly so if such a company achieves a monopoly of a single market, say the market in table grapes. It is not necessary to achieve an absolute monopoly in order to enjoy the benefits of owning one; you have only to command a large enough share of the market, say 25 percent, in order to be able to set the price for everyone.

Given the fact that the price paid the American farmer has always been low, a question might arise as to why big business would ever want to go into farming. The possibility of obtaining a monopoly and then hiking the price could be one reason for corporate intrusion into agriculture. A more compelling one could be the possibility of being paid for growing nothing, or receiving subsidies. The government subsidies, originally designed to help Grandpa stagger around his hundred acres during the Depression, are still being paid. But they are not being paid to Grandpa, who quit farming forty years ago. As Representative Peter P. Peyser, a New York member of the House Agriculture Committee says, the congressmen from the farm states still represent the farmers. But, as Representative Peyser adds, the farmers the congressmen represent are no longer so many sturdy sons of the soil, each standing tall and proud on his land, ankle-deep in mud with hayseeds coming out his ears. Today's farmers are much more likely to be corporate directors whose occasional contacts with the soil are limited to their visits to their country clubs. No farm anywhere in the country is under as intensive cultivation as are the ten square miles that are known as Washington, D.C. There, the farm hands are lobbyists sowing money and promises among congressmen and hopeful presidential candidates of both parties. These seeds burst into orchards of money trees for the corporate reapers of such strange fruits as windfalls, tax dodges, and subsidies. It is a thought to take with us on our next visit to our friendly neighborhood supermarket.

Another thought was expressed by a witness before a Senate committee. He asked the senators to think about Thanksgiving.

"The Smithfield ham," he said, "comes from ITT, the turkey is a product of Greyhound Corporation, the lettuce comes from Dow Chemical Company, the potatoes are provided by the Boeing Company, and Tenneco brought the fresh fruits and vegetables. The applesauce is made available by American Brands, while both Coca-Cola and Royal Crown Cola have provided the fruit juices."

Green Tomatoes and Dead Yellow Birds

Not every farm in the country is owned by a corporation, or leased to one, or rented to one. The huge farms that produce the bulk of the nation's foodstuffs are, however, very much a part of corporate life, hooked into nationwide marketing and distributive systems, and they operate according to the methods that apply elsewhere in a mass-producing, mass-consuming society. With nearly 90 percent of Americans living in cities, it is perhaps inevitable that this should be the case. Whether these methods serve human ends as well as they serve commercial ones is another matter. Farmer Jones would say no.

Jones was a man who raised beans. It was his dream to win first prize at the state fair. Of course he wanted to make money. Who does not? In his simple way, Farmer Jones thought if he raised the best beans, those beans would make him the most money. In this line of thinking, his first allegiance was to himself. He took pride in producing high quality beans. As long as he did that, he thought, the money would take care of itself.

Corporation Company's attitude was, the hell with the state fair. All Corporation Company wanted was to make money, and it figured it could make it by producing the most beans at the least cost in order to grab a percentage of the national bean market in order to influence the price of that market. So Corporation Company bought a hundred square miles of prime bean land, only to find Farmer Jones's hundred acres sitting smack in the middle of them.

Farmer Jones wouldn't sell out, even at the good price Corporation Company offered him. Nor would he lease or rent his land, or become a contract farmer to the company. It seemed he wanted to stay on his own land, raising his own beans.

Well, sir, first thing you know, Farmer Jones found his prize beans undersold at the market. The commission agent, a creature of Corporation Company, gave him a price below the cost of raising those beans.

Next thing you know, when Farmer Jones went to the bank for a loan to tide him over until the next crop, the bank said no.

Guess who the bank's biggest customer was?

Farmer Jones still did not catch on, and went to court

about it. He wound up in bankruptcy, listening to the sheriff auctioning off his furniture. If you want to poke through records in California courts, as William Robbins did in the course of research for his book, you, too, can read all about this sort of thing. For some reason, we worship size in America, and take a kind of pride in thinking of big business as engaged in cutthroat competition. Maybe it is because we like to sit up late watching throats being cut on television.

Apart from rural throat-slashing, corporate intrusion into agriculture has had a certain man-grinding effect, which can very well affect the land itself. Let us look at it this way:

A thousand acres is a thousand acres, and that's a fact. So much land can produce so many beans, and that is another fact. The same number of beans could be grown by ten men using a variety of machines, or by a hundred men groveling around in the dirt on their hands and knees, using their fingers. If Corporation Company owns the whole spread and hires ten men to use company machines to tend it, then not the land or the machines or the beans would mean a thing in the world to those employees. For all they care, the land can dry up, the machines can break, and the beans can rot. All they care about is the paycheck, and the only people they need to know, or to have anything to do with, are the foreman and the cashier, who are employees like themselves. The whole lot of them might as well be working in a city factory. And that can make quite a difference to the land, because the way a man does his work reflects his opinion of his job and of himself. The botched and incomplete automobiles coming off Detroit assembly lines perfectly reflect the morale of the workers and what the workers think of their employers and the product. If corporate field hands take the same attitude, their lack of concern can botch the crop if not the field as well.

For instance, if they notice that the tractors are unduly

impacting the land, it might not occur to them, or even to their foreman, to suggest that the company might look around for lighter equipment or new methods. They would be more likely to think it none of their business, because when people are organized in a quasi-military way, as people in businesses and factories often are, each person becomes responsible only for following his instructions in his fractional task, trusting or believing or even being ordered to believe, that someone wiser than he is in control of the overall operation. For that matter, the men on the tractors might never check the oil in the bases of their engines, reasoning that it is the responsibility of the mechanics in the motor pool to do so. Likewise, if they should entertain suspicions about the quality or even the health of the beans they are raising, they might again believe it none of their business. The beans, after all, do not belong to them.

On the other hand, if ten men each owned a hundred of the thousand acres, the little they owned would be of first importance to them. They would have an intense concern for the health of the land itself and for the quality of their produce. Their relationship with one another might well be one of rivalry, or it could be one of camaraderie and mutual assistance. Moreover, not all of them might grow beans, much less the same kind or quality of beans. Some might, instead, grow different crops, with the result that the thousand acres would represent a varied garden that would be more important to the nearest townsfolk than a thousand acres of beans would be. In any case, the relationship of each man to his land, and of the men to one another, and the relationship of farmers to consumers would be far more intimate and within the human tradition than is the case with Corporation Company and its concern for mass production for some anonymous national bean market. Whatever might be said for the virtues of mass production must always be measured against the resultant loss to the variety and quality of human life, as well as against the loss of variety and quality in the product.

But more than this, there is no reason to believe that our modern mass-production farming methods are as efficient as the corporate farmers would have us believe. For example, the Chinese feed a population four times larger than our own, and they do this on much less farm acreage than we have under cultivation. The Chinese are self-sufficient with respect to food supplies, and the foods they produce are various and excellent, and their cuisine is as distinguished as it is subtle. Credit for this need not be given the contemporary Chinese government, for such was the case in Marco Polo's time, too. For thousands of years the Chinese have been well aware of man's relationship to the soil and have worked out a relationship that suits their needs. It is a horsecollar and hand-labor one, practiced on small parcels of land, and it provides relatively more food per acre, of greater variety, than does our mechanized and incorporated big business agriculture. Much the same thing may be said of Western Europe, even though Europe imports some of its foodstuffs. A great many of the foods and wines of Europe are famous throughout the world, being produced in sufficient supply to be exported, and they are produced by hand labor on parcels of land that are relatively the size of postage stamps when compared with American farms. Indeed, in providing the populace with plenty of good things to eat, hand-labor and horsecollar America was more productive than jet-age America now is. A question, therefore, certainly arises as to whether we really need all our modern apparatus of gigantic mechanized farms, processing businesses, automated distribution systems, and national supermarket chains — particularly when the ultimate product of all this corporate claptrap is worse food of less variety at ever higher prices.

To farm on the largest possible scale is a splendid idea, but the thing to know is the area of the possible. Beyond a certain point, growth may be not good but cancerous. The point can be illustrated thus:

In a matter of minutes, a small biplane can drench a hundred square miles with a pesticide guaranteed to kill almost every bug there is. The cost of renting such a machine and hiring a pilot is far lower than the cost of hiring gangs of laborers to do the same job. It is also easier, cheaper, and less time-consuming to spray the whole countryside than it would be to find out which bugs are damaging which crops so that you could introduce to your fields the natural enemies of the bugs that are doing the damage.

Now let us say the hundred square miles include bushes, trees, and watercourses as well as open fields. To the airplane, this makes no difference. It skims along; the spray streams out, billows, and drifts over the entire area. End of the bug problem. If you own those hundred square miles, this should make you very happy. You have brought modern methods and good old American know-how to a big job — and you've cleaned it up in no time at all at almost no cost. Your crops are safe from bugs.

But there may be a few little problems. The lowing herd upon the poisoned lea will pass the stuff along to thee. The pesticide may reappear in the milk and meat. The birds in the bushes and trees, the fish in the streams, and the frogs on the banks that eat the poisoned bugs may die, and that's a pity because they all have a vital part to play in nature's food chain and system of balances. As a result of your tampering with nature's system, you learn that you may have begun to destroy the land itself.

Now let us say you fertilize your fields each year with synthetic fertilizers. By such means you can, apparently, never exhaust the land; you can keep all your fields in constant production. This surely makes much more economic sense than the rather feudal habit of allowing fields to lie fallow in order to rehabilitate themselves. Unfortunately, there once again may be some little problems.

For example, every time it rains, some of the fertilizer runs off the land, or finds its way into ground water and so into the streams, where it could touch off an explosive growth of algae and weeds, with resultant damage to the animal life in the streams and to the potability of the water. Great rivers are by no means immune. Algae and weeds are beginning to clog even the broad, deep St. Lawrence River, and some of the scientists who are looking into the problem say they believe that synthetic fertilizers are the major source of the phosphates that are causing this growth; that city wastes, including household detergents, play only a minor part. The case against these fertilizers has not been established beyond all possible doubt, but one thing can be said: No such pollution took place in all the centuries when human or animal manure was used as fertilizer on the single-family general farms. But such farms are nearly as extinct as whooping cranes, and farmers who have no livestock to fertilize their fields must use synthetic compounds. Given the choice, they might use them anyway, because the synthetic fertilizers are less noisome and more easily handled than manure.

Questions arise as to who cares. A corporate conglomerate that owns an agricultural division that farms hundreds of square miles is not apt to be responsive to a complaint that its farming methods may be poisoning people, destroying the balance of nature, and polluting the water. The corporation is more likely to say that the cases against pesticides and synthetic fertilizers have yet to be proved, and there will be considerable merit in this contention. The fact that something kills laboratory rats does not always mean that it will kill people. So far, no one has been sufficiently cold-blooded to run a fifty-year controlled experiment with ten thousand human beings, feeding half of them from birth on substances suspected of being harmful, and feeding the other half on substances known to be healthful. Likewise, the nation has not yet lived long enough to see whether certain long-range predictions, made with respect to upsetting nature's balances, will actually prove to be correct. If a corporation should argue along these lines, it has every right to do so. The corporation has an investment to protect. So, for that matter, has every farmer, large or small. It is unrealistic to ask anyone, and particularly a $4 billion corporation, to stop whatever it is doing just because someone suspects it might prove to be harmful, especially when equally competent testimony can be had to the contrary and when the entire question is hypothetical. It may be dismaying, but it should not be surprising, to find huge corporations hiring lobbyists and assembling scientists to refute the critics of their practices. There is no evil here. If you and I were threatened with a court action, we should certainly want to hire the best available lawyers to present the best evidence in our defense. But there is a danger. The danger is that, since money talks and the most money talks the loudest, the sound of big money shouting could drown out the voices of those who, after the damage has been done, will be seen to have been correct.

The most impressive effect of our application of a high technology and big business methods to agriculture is that so few of us produce such astonishingly large amounts of food. In fact, we produce so much more than we can eat that we can afford to sell or give thousands of tons of it to less fortunate lands. There are those who say America can and should be the principal grocer to the world, and there is something to this agrument. We might, however, produce even more food for the world if, like the Chinese, the Europeans, and the earlier Americans, we had more farmers on the land, cultivating smaller parcels. Nevertheless, it is impressive to think of how much is produced by so few. It is next quite depressing to realize what a scanty variety these few offer us, and how poor the quality is. Let us take lettuce, for example.

Say you are a lettuce grower. You probably grow lettuce in California, because 70 percent of America's lettuce is grown there, so the odds are seven out of ten that you are a California grower. As such, you are part of a localized, specialized industry catering to a national market that includes not only supermarket chains, but even such road-side stands as the one in competition with Mr. Bosch. You do not grow simply a few heads for yourself and the neighbors, but whole trainloads destined for people you do not know, who live as far away as Maine. You sell your trainloads to an agency that puts them into the national distribution system.

Now, what you, every other grower, the wholesale agency, and every supermarket manager knows is that most Americans prefer iceberg lettuce to any other kind. Why they prefer it may have much to do with ignorance, advertising, habit, or, perhaps, taste. For whatever reasons, iceberg lettuce is what most of them *buy*. What kind of lettuce should you raise? If you have any doubts about this, the wholesale agency will be glad to resolve them for you. If you want to deal in the national market, you are going to have to raise iceberg lettuce even if you can't stand the sight or taste of it yourself.

Let us now say you are a supermarket manager. You sell lettuce to thousands of customers every week, most of whom buy iceberg lettuce — never mind why. What kind of lettuce should you stock? Your produce bins are only so large and you have allotted only so much space in those bins for lettuce. Moreover, produce is perishable. Iceberg lettuce stands shipping well; the heads you receive have already traveled two thousand miles and are still in fairly good shape, or if they are not, you simply pull off a few outside leaves, spray the heads with water, advertise a special on "fresh lettuce" — and raise the price. If customers come in, asking if you have any other kinds of lettuce, you tell them no, there is little demand for whatever other kind they have in mind. What do you care for those oddballs? You have thousands of customers, all of them total strangers; you are the only supermarket serving a large, populous area; and you could not possibly run a supermarket that catered to individual tastes. That would be a contradiction in terms. So you stock only the lettuce that most people buy. The fact that this is a hedge against spoilage is an additional reason why you do so. Because you are a part of a national marketing system you buy California iceberg lettuce because that is what the system sends you, and because you are a part of this system you cannot and do not buy whatever fresh lettuce might appear in season in your area.

The grower, the supermarket manager, and none of the men in the middle deals with people. All deal instead with numbers. If you are the customer, you do not deal with people, either. You deal with a system. Of course there are many exceptions, but the rule is, if you buy at a supermarket and intend to have a salad tonight, you are probably going to have to make it out of a wilting California cannonball whether you like it or not.

You would like a few tomatoes in your salad? Well, now, 65 percent of America's tomatoes are grown in California. They have a year-round growing season out there, it seems, which is why so much of our produce comes from California and why the corporations engaged in agriculture have so heavily invested in that state's land. So the odds are that your tomatoes will be California ones. The reason why they do not taste like tomatoes is that they are not, strictly speaking, tomatoes. They might have become tomatoes had anyone allowed them to ripen naturally, acquiring not only taste but also the nutrient value of vine-ripened tomatoes. There are as you know several varieties of tomatoes, but there is likely to be only one kind offered at your supermarket. It will be a variety grown not for its taste or value, but to withstand mechanical pickers; that is why its hide is elephantine. The reason why it tastes like tough, damp balsa wood is because it was mechanically picked while it was hard and green, so that it would arrive unrotten at a store two thousand miles away. Its red color owes nothing to sunshine. While in transit, it was treated with ethylene gas. The reasons why you cannot find several varieties of vine-ripened tomatoes in your supermarket are the same reasons why you cannot find several varieties of fresh-picked lettuce there. You are dealing with a mass-marketing system, and you are discovering what my friend meant when he said the shoddy always drives the good out of a mass market.

There are plenty of people, not all of them farmers or otherwise in the food business, who believe the system is a good thing. Their argument is that the system makes it possible for people all over the continent to enjoy a variety of fresh produce no matter what the season. It is closer to the mark to say that people all over the continent are given the opportunity to buy a limited variety of foodstuffs that lack the freshness, flavor, and nutritive value of locally grown seasonal produce.

That the system does not really offer variety may be seen everywhere in the supermarket. Would you like berries for dessert? The chances are that you will not find whortleberries, gooseberries, loganberries, boxberries, gingerberries, checkerberries, elderberries, mulberries, or even red or black raspberries at your Giant Plastic Food Store. America produces them, but the system does not. All you will probably find are hothouse strawberries, which taste sort of damp and pink, or big squashy blueberries, which taste like nothing in particular. Nuts? Do you see any chinquapins, butternuts, English walnuts, or filberts in the store? If you want a ham for dinner, it is unlikely that you will have a choice among brine-cured, pepper-cured, hickory-smoked or corncob-smoked ham, or among hams taken from pigs raised on acorns or on peanuts. America could produce all sorts of hams, and once did, but now the system most usually offers us just one kind. It will be from a too-young, too-fat-too-soon corn-fed hog, injected with smoke-flavored water, and part of your fun in eating it will be the joy you realize in having paid ham prices for water.

The examples could be multiplied, but only to the point of the further detailing of an American tragedy. Our continent once upon a time produced a tremendous variety of food-stuffs, for the reason that food, be it animal or vegetable, is a product of the soil as affected by the climate, and our continent possesses every sort of soil, geography, and climate known in the temperate zone, and in the subtropical and subarctic zones.

Now, within any region, variety is once again possible. Wholly apart from the variety of kinds of pears that may be grown on the side of a hill, the pears grown on one side of it may be subtly different from those grown on the other — because of differences, however slight, in the amounts of sun, wind, and rainfall. What cows eat can flavor their milk. So can the water they drink. Sheep grazing on salt marshes taste different from sheep grazed on inland grasses. So, too, there is a difference in the taste of grass-fed and corn-fed cattle, just as there are differences in flavor among hogs raised on different foods. In addition to these natural differences, the kind of care that different people give their crops and animals can make a difference in the taste and quality of those crops and animals. Still further differences can be created by the cook in the kitchen. Catsup, for instance, means any liquid relish. There could be as many different catsups as there are cooks in kitchens, none of whom use tomatoes in the concoction of catsup. Given a nation that occupies a continent capable of producing almost any kind of food, and given a population of some two hundred fifty million people representative of virtually every race and nation on earth, one might reasonably expect gastronomic and agricultural miracles. Surely the last thing anyone should expect would be standard brands, diminished variety, and deliberately lowered quality.

The land, our fabulous continent, still exists. The fact that it no longer brings forth its infinite variety is because we have left the land in search of values other than those of the fruits of the earth, these having to do with other things that money can buy; because we have been pushed off the land and into cities by the power of the money generated by a society predicated on mass production for mass consumption; because the use of the land has been rationalized to serve the needs of the society we have created. All of this is very different from other human societies, including an earlier American one, wherein it was the nature of the land that shaped the lives of the people — not the other way around.

We have now been off the land long enough to have produced a generation that has no knowledge of the appearance, taste, or nutritive quality of natural foods, as compared with the appearance, taste, and quality of some rather less than natural ones. Most Americans born in 1945 will be at least the second, if not the third, urban generation. Their lack of knowledge, combined with the dynamics inherent in

modern agricultural and marketing methods, is one of the
reasons why Frank Perdue was able to become the presiding
genius of a $90 million corporate empire.

Philadelphians first became aware of Frank Perdue when,
in 1974, a skinny, bald, countrified fellow appeared on
television together with a dead bird. He had a message for
the folks. That was his chicken he had there, and you could
see for yourself how yellow it was. That yellow color was
how you could tell when a chicken was good and healthy
— and good tender eating. Now, he was a chicken farmer.
He'd been a chicken farmer all his life. He knew. He would
never sell you folks the kind of pale, stale birds that other
people did. He'd never put his personal tag on a chicken if it
wasn't the best, most tender chicken there was. He was an
honest man who took pride in his work. It takes a tough man
to raise a tender chicken. Every one of his birds you saw in
the store would have his personal tag on it, or it wouldn't be
in the store.

Some people thought these advertisements were the fun-
niest things on television. They never imagined that the
straight-talking old bumpkin with the dead yellow bird was
actually a farmer, much less that he was actually Frank
Perdue himself. They thought an advertising agency had
cleverly found a man who looked a bit like a chicken to pose
with a chicken — like the dog food advertisement that
showed dog owners who looked like their dogs. But those
who laughed did not necessarily question the truth of the
advertisement. Most city people had no idea how to tell one
dead chicken from another for the very good reason that they
had never raised chickens themselves. The reason why
people were ready to believe the advertisement could very
well be that they hoped it was true: there was now a bird on
the market that would prove to be better than the chickens
they had heretofore found in the stores. For whatever reason

— the impression of honesty or the hope of something better — ignorant Philadelphians responded to the advertisements to such an extent that at least one supermarket manager was led by public demand to stock his poultry counter with nothing other than Perdue chickens.

If Philadelphians were late to meet Frank Perdue on television, this is because the advertising campaign had only then opened in their area. It was first launched in the New York market area, and in the Boston-Providence-Worcester one, with such success that by the time Frank Perdue opened in Philadelphia he was selling chickens at the very tidy rate of one and a half million birds a week. And that was quite a change from the days when his father, Arthur Perdue, had started out in the chicken business in 1920 with fifty Leghorns, selling table eggs.

According to *Food Engineering* magazine,* Frank dropped out of Salisbury State College to join the family business in Maryland's Delmarva peninsula in 1939, adding New Hampshire Reds to the then two thousand birds in the family flock, and over the years the business grew to include hatching and raising broilers as well as selling eggs. Toward the end of the 1960s, it occurred to Frank Perdue that Perdue, Inc., could sell a lot more chickens if he could only find a way of making his chickens *seem* to be different from other companies' chickens. He found out that marigold petals added to chicken feed will turn the birds' skins yellow. Now all he had to do was convince the public that a bird with a yellow skin was better and healthier and more tender than a chicken with a pale skin, so he went shopping for an advertising agency that would help him get this message across to the most people at the least cost. He came up with Scali, McCabe and Cloves of New York. The agency suggested that Perdue

* The September 1974 issue.

himself appear on television to give his own forceful impression of Frank Perdue, the chicken farmer.

As Frank Perdue and the agency will be the very first to say, the addition of yellow color has not the slightest effect, of any sort whatsoever, upon the health, quality, tenderness, or taste of the chicken. It does, however, have everything to do with the fact that Perdue sales tripled, and this in turn has everything to do with why Perdue, Inc., now spends $1 million a year to add marigold petals to its chicken feed. *Food Engineering* calls this "a clever merchandising idea . . . one of the food industry's most stunning recent successes." Millions of housewives, the magazine said, "believe his no-nonsense claims of quality, and tripled his sales as a reward."

Another way of looking at it is to say that Frank Perdue is taking advantage of public ignorance to make people believe he is giving them something he is not giving them. In this, however, he has plenty of company among his corporate colleagues down on the farm, such as those California tomato growers who send to market something that is not precisely what it seems to be, and other chicken-battery operators who produce something that is not entirely a chicken.

Since it is the modern chicken-battery that forced farmers like Hiram Bosch out of the chicken business, and since the battery birds are all that we can find in our supermarkets today, and since battery birds bear only a casual resemblance to real chickens, and finally because a battery operation encapsulates corporate efforts in agriculture, let us pause for a moment to enjoy, shall we say, a bird's eye view.

Maturity is the optimum state of any animal or vegetable. Ripeness is all. The taste and the nutritive value of the flesh of any animal, including the chicken, is directly related to what the animal eats, how it lives, and how old it is. The piggiest pig you can possibly eat will be the mature wild boar, which leads a true pig's life in a forest, not a hog's life in a sty. The boar will have comparatively little fat on him, which is also true of wild ducks or any other animals that have grown to maturity in the freedom and circumstances that nature intended. They will be precisely as fat or as lean as need be. Large human populations cannot, however, be maintained on the basis of wild foods; cultivation and animal husbandry are essential. The entire aim and purpose of these efforts should be to bring our crops and animals to a state of maturity under those conditions that best enable the crops and animals to fulfill their maximum potentiality as food.

With respect to chicken-raising, the idea ought to be to produce the most chickenlike chicken you possibly can. You cannot of course raise chickens in a state of nature; you must keep them safe in a henyard. But within the henyard they should be reasonably free to do what it is that chickens naturally do, such as run about, squawk, scratch, chase bugs, flap their wings, and otherwise exercise from egg to chopping block for the more than three months it takes for the watery flesh of the chick to become the firmer and more nourishing and tasty flesh of the pullet. In addition to chicken feed, chickens need space and time in order to become the chickens they are capable of becoming. And this is what you would give them if you wanted to raise chickens.

You would do nothing of the sort if, however, you wanted to make money. The economics of modern chicken farming require you to operate a factory rather than a henyard. You must have at least sixty thousand birds, each crammed into a tiny cage in a fully automated, artificially lighted, air-conditioned, antiseptic, and temperature-controlled chicken prison. Without once ever venturing outdoors or seeing the light of day, chickens are hatched, fattened, killed, plucked, dressed, frozen, and wrapped by machine in their marvelous mechanical chicken prison, where almost nothing — except taste and quality — is lost in the process. From egg to death, each bird enjoys a life of solitary and immobile confinement: measured amounts of a compound of organic foods and synthetic chemicals, selected to put the most weight on the birds in the least time at the lowest cost, are dribbled automatically into the cages. An immobile pullet fed in a battery will bloat up to a salable weight many weeks before a scratching barnyard bird would come to that weight, but with the difference that the young bloater's flesh will be tasteless and watery, thanks to its tasteless and unnatural diet, its unnatural immobility, and its immaturity; whereas the flesh of the naturally ranging and mature bird will be firm, nourishing, and will taste like chicken. Two billion watery bloaters are sold in the United States every year, for the simple reason that no other kind is available in your friendly neighborhood supermarket, because no one can raise chickens naturally, in sufficient quantity to meet the system's demands, and remain in business against the cheap, mass-produced battery birds. Research in the poultry industry is continuing, centering on the problem of how to reduce further the time and cost necessary to produce a pound of all too, too pallid pullet flesh.

"Cost to produce a pound of meat," Frank Perdue explained to *Food Engineering*. "That's what it's all about."

And that indeed is what it is all about if you are raising and selling a product, not a chicken.

Sometimes, despite all the marvels wrought by automated machinery, the product arrives in the poultry counter without the full number of its parts. You may or may not find the neck stuffed into the carcass cavity; the bag that should contain the edible entrails may contain the gizzard, but not the heart or liver. The right wing may be missing, sheared off by the dressing-out machine. I once inspected a poultry counter full of frozen chickens wrapped in plastic, and discovered the right wing missing from every one of them. There are two possible explanations of these phenomena. One is that machines might make mistakes. The other is that somebody is doing a brisk business in necks, wings, and giblets at the chicken buyer's expense. If so, perhaps that, too, might be called "a clever merchandising idea" by those who think the proper spelling of chicken is "chicane."

The argument for the chicken-battery is the argument for all other forms of mass production for mass consumption: to rationalize agricultural production on the largest scale is to provide the most food to the most people at the least cost to the farmer. Theoretically, the saving in cost will also be passed on to the consumer, but that is only a theory. It is more to the point to say that the rationalization of agriculture on the largest scale results in our producing a great deal of food that is not as good to eat, or as good for us to eat, as food produced on a much smaller scale can be. It is also fair to say that our highly rationalized food-producing and marketing methods result in our spending sixty cents out of every food dollar we spend at the store for that which is not food at all, but which represents the cost of the system itself — the cost of .processing, wrapping, transporting, and marketing our foodstuffs, as well as the cost of telling ourselves through advertising that what we are buying is really better than it actually is.

Hey, Diddle Diddle, the Men in the Middle

More Is Lost in the Process

When food leaves the corporate farm, its price increases every step of the way to the supermarket. Freshness, nutrients, and taste may be lost en route, but in any case the price goes up. This difference in price, between what the farmer receives at the farm gate and what we pay at the checkout counter, is technically known as the farm-retail spread. In 1974, the Department of Agriculture estimated the spread to average out at sixty cents. The farmer received forty cents; we paid one dollar; and somebody else ran off with sixty cents of our food money.

Congressional hearings were held in an effort to find out just who this somebody was, because crazy things seemed to be happening. As Representative Joseph P. Vigorito of Pennsylvania said with respect to meat prices, we "seem to have an increase in 1973 of double what many consumers thought was an outrageous increase in 1972," and in 1974, when Representative Vigorito opened hearings into the matter, store prices were rising to new records while farm prices were falling. Cattlemen were receiving less for their animals than the cost of raising them, and the price of steak at the store rose to such heights that citizens were organizing boycotts against beef. Normally, one would suppose that store prices would fall if farm prices did. The fact that the very reverse was happening, and that the farm-retail spread was widening, was the reason for the hearings.

The congressmen soon learned that, as Representative Paul Findley of Illinois put it, "it is in the off-farm chain of events that the consumer is now taking a beating." They also learned that most of the links of that chain were middlemen. "And it's not just middlemen," said Representative Peyser of New York, "because the middlemen have middlemen on *them.*"

But it was not only the men in the middle who were making the price of food go up. Some of the fault lay in the intricacy of the American system itself, a system so delicately balanced that if you touch a corner of it here, something else happens in another corner way over there. For instance, the government reduced highway speed to fifty-five miles an hour in order to save oil. Oil *was* saved, but the carrying capacity of trucks was reduced by 30 percent, which raised hell with the trucking industry — and also increased the price of food trucked to market. In such a system, when the price of anything goes up, all other prices are affected.

A corollary of this rule is, the fewer people there are to handle a product, and the less any of them have to do to it to ready it for market, the less vulnerable that product is to a general inflation. Simply put, if a farmer picks an apple from a tree and hands it to you, he may indeed charge you for his labor and the cost of growing the apple, but he will not also charge you for any rising costs of packing, wrapping, advertising, and trucking, or for any of the costs of heating, lighting, staffing, and renting a store. All those operations are the provinces of middlemen, who, as Representative Peyser says, may well have middlemen on them, in the form of commission agents, brokers, and speculators in commodity and crop futures.

Other middlemen, the food processors, add things to food while sometimes subtracting natural flavor and nutritional value, and the profit they make from their activities is added to the price of the food as it passes through their hands on the way to the store.

All that I have been discussing applies to that simplest and most basic of foods, the loaf of bread. In 1972, a loaf of sliced white bread sold in New York City for thirty-three cents, and by 1974 the price of that same loaf of bread had nearly doubled. It sold at sixty-one cents. What made the price go up, and who got the money? Well, let's begin down on the corporate farm, where Agrozap, Inc., grows wheat.

In 1974, Agrozap sold wheat for $5.00 a bushel. In 1972 the company had received $1.20 a bushel, but Agrozap was a special exception to the rule that said farm prices were falling in those years. It was one of the very few beneficiaries, other than grain brokers, of a stupendous, ill-advised, and possibly crooked deal made by the Nixon administration with the Soviet Union, whereby America emptied its granary to Russia at the taxpayers' expense, with the result that the price of wheat quadrupled. A federal adventure in diplomacy therefore had something to do with doubling the price of bread in New York. But not everything; there were others involved.

Agrozap sold its bushel of wheat to the proprietor of a grain elevator, who added his profitable storage and handling charges to it before shipping it to a flour mill. The cost of storing, handling, and shipping had now been added to the bushel, and somewhere in these costs were the salaries of office managers, clerks, laborers, railroad personnel, and the prices of Diesel fuel, electricity, light bulbs, paper, typewriters. And on and on the costs would run through the entire social fabric.

Now the miller takes that bushel of wheat in hand. He first strips the wheat of its husk and germ, which contain the vitamins, minerals, and proteins that make wheat nourishing. He may sell this bran as animal feed.

Next, by a complicated chemical process, the miller converts what remains of the wheat into a bleached flour that is largely starch. This product contains so little that is nourishing that insects ignore it and rats perish if fed on it. But this is the flour that goes to the corporate baker whose giant concern produces millions of loaves. (If the flour you see at the store is called "enriched," the word means that the miller, having subtracted some twenty vitamins, minerals, and proteins from the wheat, has then added four or five synthetic ones to the flour. More accurately, the flour should be called "deprived," because its nutrient value is well below that of freshly ground wheat. If anyone has been enriched by this process, it is the miller, whose processing adds at least twenty cents to the bushel of wheat converted to the starchy flour that goes to the housewife.)

Rather than rage against the quality of the flour it receives from the miller, the corporate baker, Humble Pie Farms, Inc., is delighted with it. This is because Humble Pie Farms can add more water to starch than it can add to wheat; thus more loaves of bread can be made of the starchy flour than could be made of the same amount of whole wheat flour.

Humble Pie Farms can make seventy twenty-two ounce loaves from the miller's flour, which is derived from Agrozap's bushel of wheat, at a cost in flour of eight cents a loaf.

To the flour and water, Humble Pie Farms adds (and I quote from a label) "sugar, shortening, salt, dairy solids, yeast, dough conditioner, yeast food, sodium propionate, enriched with niacin, iron sulphate, thiamine hydrochloride, riboflavin." The label does not specify whatever a "dough conditioner" might be, or of what the "yeast food" consists. The sodium propionate is a compound that retards the spoilage of the other ingredients, so that the bread will appear to remain fresh for a week. The remaining ingredients represent the bakery's "enrichment" of the anemic starch it bought from the miller; they are token restorations of some of the vitamins and minerals that were taken out of the wheat by the milling process.

What emerges from the corporate baker's oven is not precisely bread. It is something that John L. Hess has happily described as "a ghastly cloud of sugared chemistry," and this is sliced, wrapped first in a waxed paper bearing a printed label, and next in a plastic bag secured by a twist of coated wire, and it is then trucked either directly to the supermarket or to a firm that buys it and then trucks and sells it to a supermarket. In either event, the wholesale price of the loaf of bread is, or in 1974 was in New York City, 48.5 cents.

This wholesale price represents Humble Pie Farms' profit, plus the cost of the miller's flour and its shipment to the bakery, and the costs of all the ingredients the bakery added to the flour, together with the costs of baking, slicing, wrapping once and wrapping twice, advertising and marketing, the maintenance costs of the bakery, taxes on the business and the property, the salaries of all manner of employees, and the costs and profits of all the manufacturers and suppliers of waxed-paper bags, plastic bags, and twists of paper-covered wire.

Once arrived in the supermarket, the loaf of bread is marked up by 20 percent. The supermarket's explanation is that it must add 12.2 cents to every loaf it buys in order to cover its operating costs and earn a profit.

Now you will recall that Agrozap, Inc., received $5.00 for its bushel of wheat, from which enough flour was derived to enable the bakery to make seventy loaves of bread, which were sold in the store for sixty-one cents apiece. Therefore, $5.00 worth of wheat became $42.70 worth of sliced bread on the way from farm to table, and that is one of the highest-priced spreads you are likely to find in the food business. The $37.70 in the middle represents all the things that happened to a bushel of wheat between farm and store, and one of the things that happened was that virtually all of the nourishment was taken out of it.

It is indeed strange to think that in America the nutritional value of a basic food can be reduced to nearly zero while its price can be increased more than eight times, but, to borrow an advertising man's phrase, That's the way it crumbles, Cooky. In America, you can pay out $42.70 for seventy loaves of bread, and instead of giving you bread for your money, the supermarket hands you 140 bags containing seventy squishy oblongs of sliced library paste, made in a chemical factory a week ago and a hundred miles away.

Argument on a Hilltop

None of the businessmen who stand in line between the farm gate and the dinner table is in any way responsible for the rising cost of food. If you do not believe this, you have only to ask one, and he will say "Nossir, it's not me." He and his confreres have said this to congressmen, to representatives of consumer groups, and to such private citizens as myself. It would seem that no one received a living wage in 1974 for whatever he did to turn our bushel of wheat into that loaf of sliced bread.

The millers told congressional committees that between 1972 and 1974 their milling costs more than doubled, but their profits did not.

The bakers' lobby in Washington, the American Bakers Association, said that every part of the production process, including the price of plastic bags, had increased in cost. Meanwhile, the ABA said, their profit margins had shrunk to the point where the corporate baker made only .0084 cents' profit on every loaf sold. The price of shortening increased 80 percent in two years, they said, and that of sugar rose 300 percent. Of course neither shortening nor sugar is a necessary ingredient in the baking of bread, which for at least a thousand years has been made of flour, water, yeast, and salt, but never mind that: the corporate bakers did use shortening and sugar, and the price of those ingredients did indeed rise between 1972 and 1974.

Next to Capitol Hill came the supermarket people with their sad story. They contended their profits were so paper-thin that it was a wonder they were still in business.

So, with a hey, diddle, diddle, all the men in the middle said the cost of everything they bought and did was going up and up while their margins of profit were going down and down, and none of this was their fault. They, like all of us, were the victims of inflation, they said, and inflation was the government's fault.

The price of wheat shot up as a result of the government's grain deal with Russia, and that, too, was the government's fault — certainly not theirs. It was not they who had lighted off a rocket and sent the price of sugar to the moon. Somebody else, they said, was responsible for everything.

Representative Peyser of the House Agriculture Committee listened to the middlemen's testimony with a singularly dry eye. He said that a study he had made of the food industry led him to wonder if the high food prices in the supermarkets were not the result of deliberate price-rigging by the supermarket chains.

The congressman's doubts were shared in the upper chamber by Senator William Proxmire, who had also been conducting an investigation into the food industry. Senator Proxmire suspected that middlemen in the food business were responsible for no less than two thirds of the very inflation about which they were complaining. The senator spoke of "immense and unjustified price increases" in the nation's supermarkets. He said his preliminary investigations showed that "concentration is on the rise in processing and retailing, and the result apparently is a lack of competition, administered prices, and monopoly profits. A healthy dose of antitrust [action] is the remedy." He added that if we really want to get food prices down, "the target has to be the uncompetitive structure of the food industry itself."

This was also the view of the Justice Department, where there are fourteen cases pending against food companies at the time of this writing, each alleging violations of the antitrust laws, and at least twenty more such cases are under investigation.

At the Treasury Department, Secretary William Simon said the White House Policy Board was indeed concerned about the profits being made by middlemen in the food business and about the possibility that they might be unjustly enriching themselves at the public's expense.

The concentration of interests to which both Representative Peyser and Senator Proxmire referred had also attracted the attention of the Federal Trade Commission, which discovered that, in the last twenty-five years, twenty-four giant corporate conglomerates had swallowed up more than a hundred food companies whose corporate assets had totaled $7 billion. Fifty corporations, the FTC said, account for 60 percent of all assets in the food-processing industry and 61 percent of the profits; 40 percent of all retail food sales in the country are shared by just four supermarket chains. Such a concentration of money and power, an FTC economist told a joint congressional committee, creates a monopoly situation rather similar to that which now prevails in the automobile and steel businesses. In a monopoly situation, competition could be killed off, markets could be shared, and prices could be rigged.

While the middlemen make their denials and the congressmen entertain their suspicions, we might reflect that food means life to the people who eat it, whereas it means money to the people who grow it, process it, and market it. Food would therefore seem to be a public necessity, and if we can all agree that it certainly is, then a question arises as to whether the food industry should not be regarded as a public utility, and, next, whether that industry should not be just as subject to government regulation as any other public utility. So far, no one to my knowledge has put the question just this way in Congress, but every congressional investigation and every antitrust action is a step preliminary to asking that question.

The price of food at the farm and the price of it at the store are two entirely different things, and, it seems, no necessary relationship exists between them. Farm prices can and do go down while store prices can and do go up, and one of the reasons why store prices go up is simply that the store can and does mark them up. Another reason is that the processors and distributors can and do raise the prices they charge the store. This is particularly true when a major processing company at once controls the prices it pays for the food it processes — and also owns the store.

Once food leaves the fields, it is no longer part of a food chain. It becomes part of a money chain instead. If, at the end of this money chain, a large number of people cannot afford to buy food at the store, as is indeed now the case, then the issuance of federal food stamps is a palliative, but not a cure for the problem. Here, one begins to wonder just what the problem is. Does the American way of life necessarily produce a great many people who cannot afford to buy food? Government officials sometimes speak of "desirable levels" of unemployment, although it may be doubted that all of the unemployed uniformly regard their condition as the fulfillment of their deepest desires. Congressmen are quite properly asking whether middlemen are responsible for rising food prices, and if so, to what extent. With equal justification, they might wonder how many middlemen are actually necessary to the production, distribution, and marketing of the food we must eat.

In a way, it all seems rather sad and silly, and no one's fault at all. If a successful farmer buys up his less fortunate neighbor's land, or otherwise finds an opportunity to increase his holdings, he is not necessarily an evil man. If he sells out for a good price to a large corporation, there is no necessary evil in this, either. If Greyhound Bus Lines wants to go into the turkey-raising business, why should it not? The fact that Greyhound owns the farm does not mean the turkeys will taste like oil and rubber.

We live within a system that is less of a system than it is a hodgepodge of opportunities. Everyone is trying to make a bit of money, and there is no necessary evil in that, and if some people are better at making money than other people, there is no necessary evil in that. To be sure, this systemless hodgepodge of ours permits those with the most money to make even more money, and whenever we see that this somehow seems unfair or detrimental to everyone else, then we seek some means to correct or alleviate the situation, but seldom do we suggest getting rid of the hodgepodge and replacing it with a planned use of natural resources, with a planned economy, with a completely rationalized system that would narrowly restrict our opportunities to be ourselves.

It would seem to me that the middlemen in the food business are quite right to complain of a general inflation. So do we all. It would also seem to me that a reason for inflation is the general availability of money — and the rather natural desire of any merchant to charge every penny the traffic will bear. To put it simply, if food prices rise while farm prices fall, the reason for this is that most of us have the money to pay the prices the stores ask — however unwilling we might be to have to pay these prices. At the same time, the middlemen are in a position to tell the corporate farms how little they will pay for the crops and what the stores will have to pay for the food. This is particularly true when the middleman owns the land and the stores and all the processes in between. No doubt this situation calls for remedial legislation and for the antitrust action Senator Proxmire recommends. But the middlemen are not evil. They are merely taking advantage of an opportunity to do what comes naturally. If they must be restrained by law, then we can reflect that every law is restrictive of someone's freedom, and that the sum of all laws represents our attempt to save us all from being ourselves.

Curious indeed are the things that can happen in a land of such opportunity that even the middlemen have middlemen on them, as Representative Peyser said, and one of the curious things, for which inflation could not be blamed (although opportunity could), was the dramatic rise in the price of sugar. Let us give the matter the separate attention it deserves: a section to itself.

When the Price of Sugar Cubed

In the early fall of 1974, the price of sugar in America began to rise, then gathered speed, and, like an out-bound rocket, suddenly disappeared into the heavens.

Sugar cubes, bowls of sugar, and packets of sugar vanished from American restaurant tables and cafeteria counters. Anyone who wanted sugar for his coffee had to ask for it, and he received a lump or a spoonful at a time — in at least one restaurant, from a waitress who carried the precious stuff in a holster on her belt.

In November, televised news pictures showed neighborhood bakers folding up shop because the price of sugar raised the cost of their sweetmeats beyond a point that traffic could bear.

Since sugar was the indispensable ingredient in the manufacture or preservative process of all manner of beverages and foodstuffs, the costs of all foods containing sugar were increased.

Next, the store prices of *all* foods increased, including the price of foods that contained no sugar whatsoever, because the price of sugar reached a height so dizzying that the supermarkets could not sell sugar at the price they had to pay for it. One supermarket manager opened his books to me and said, "Look for yourself. Right there: three-fifty-three. That's what it costs me. So go look at the shelf. Two-forty-nine, right? I'm giving the customer a dollar-four of my own money every time he buys sugar.

"Naturally," he said, "I got to make it up somewhere else; I mean, I can't give money away, so I have to put my prices up to cover the sugar. You see what I mean?"

Asked why he did not simply sell sugar at cost, if not at a profit, the supermarket manager threw open his arms as if to embrace the world.

"People need sugar," he said. "It's bad enough to charge two-forty-nine; I mean, I really don't like to do that to anybody. But if I charged what it costs me, three-fifty-three, nobody would believe it. People would think I was out of my mind or I was a crook or something. Listen, I tell you, the stores aren't screwing people on sugar; we're losing money on sugar."

The happiest men in America at this time were the executives of the sugar-refining companies, whose profits in the last quarter of 1974 rose between 250 and 1120 percent. "Profitability has finally come to our industry," said the $210,000-a-year president of America's largest refinery. But, he added, don't blame the refineries for the price increase. "There's no one setting the price," said one of his aides. "The price is set in the marketplace." It was the sugar growers who had driven the price sky-high, the refiners said, with the result that the refineries were now having to pay as much for raw cane as the householder had heretofore been paying for refined sugar.

"The problem on price," a Department of Agriculture spokesman said, "is that for four straight years sugar consumption has exceeded production." There was, he said, a six-million-ton shortage of sugar in America, and the rise in price reflected nothing other than obedience to "the law of supply and demand."

That's right, a refiner agreed. "When you have a product that is in short supply and valuable, you're not going to give it away."

The great sugar shortage of 1974 arrived as unexpectedly and as mysteriously as the great oil shortage, and rumors flew about that it was the Arabs who had bought up all the sugar as part of their economic holy war against the West. Reporters who tried to find out how the shortage came about and who was responsible for it were told by the Agriculture Department and the sugar refiners that the world market price was high. There had been bad growing seasons and low crop yields in the sugar-producing countries. Because sugar prices had been so low in the United States, western sugar beet farmers had stopped growing sugar beets and had turned to more valuable crops. Living standards in poor countries were rising, and as those countries became less poor, more of their people were eating more sugar. The world's population was increasing. For all these reasons a shortage existed.

This was good news to the corn-processing industry, which had developed a high fructose corn syrup that could be used as a substitute for cane and beet sugar in many food-manufacturing processes, including the production of jams, jellies, preserves, and soft drinks. The estimated market was for four and a half billion pounds of corn syrup a year. But since only one and three tenths of a billion pounds were currently being produced, it seemed very likely that the good old law of supply and demand would make the price of corn syrup scamper happily upward while plant facilities expanded, and the smart word on the corn exchange was "buy corn" — corn would jump from less than three dollars a bushel to more than five, because of what was happening in sugar.

The newspapers were by now full of advice to householders. Bake with honey instead of sugar, housewives were told. Do not try to bake with honey, housewives were told, because it will not work. No one needs sugar, a nutritionist said. It does nothing for you except give you diabetes, heart disease, and circulatory problems. If everyone stopped eating sugar, we would all be much healthier. Children do not need all that "quick energy" that sugar provides, said one nutritionist, because children nowadays are not particularly active; they don't even walk to school anymore.

While this sort of thing was being said, and while the price of sugar continued to rise, together with the prices of other foods and the price of future corn crops, and while reporters listened to people in the Agriculture Department and made notes such as "bad grng yr," "pop. expl.," "rsg dmd ex-poor," and what not, it eventually occurred to the news media to lift their eyes from America and to gaze abroad. And, lo! it appeared that the great sugar shortage was an American phenomenon. You could buy all the sugar you wanted for a few cents a pound in Mexico, as in fact many Texans were doing. You could buy sugar cheaply in Canada and elsewhere in the world. So there was no worldwide sugar shortage. It now occurred to reporters to wonder why, if there had been a shortfall of sugar in America for "four straight years," as the Agriculture Department had said, the price of sugar had not increased in any of the three prior years. Did the law of supply and demand work only once in every four years? What *was* the story? The refiners said it was the growers' fault, but the growers disagreed. Somebody, the growers said, had been speculating in sugar futures.

The operation of the futures market in crops and commodities is so arcane that even the trained lawyers who sit in Congress have difficulty understanding it. "We've had experts come in and tell us about it," Representative Peyser said, "and damned if we can figure out what the hell they're talking about. I don't think the experts understand it themselves." What did seem clear to him was that the futures market consisted of middlemen who served as agents to the middlemen who process food. Whether their agency was really necessary was quite debatable. The fact that money was made was not.

Let us suppose that you speculate in crop futures and that you are aware that more sugar can be sold in America than the suppliers of American refineries can provide. How or why you know this, I cannot say, because I can no more understand the experts than Representative Peyser could. But let us say that you have reason to know that the price of sugar in America *can* rise, and you bet that it *will.* To make the example applicable to the great sugar shortage of 1974, let us go back. In the fall of 1973 you read the futures market price quotations carefully and see that sugar is selling at eight cents a pound.

This does not refer to sugar that actually exists. It means that sugar traders, who buy from growers and sell to refineries, are willing to make a deal with growers right now: they will buy the growers' crop, which the growers have not yet planted and which will not mature and be harvested and delivered until the spring of 1975. They are willing to buy that unplanted crop right now, in the fall of 1973, at eight cents a pound. To seal the bargain, they will pay the grower 10 percent now and the rest later. At this point, the grower is out of the picture. He has sold his future crop at eight cents a pound. The future crop now belongs to the sugar trader. He is betting he can sell it for more than eight cents when he receives it.

Eight cents sounds like a good price to you. You are willing to bet the price will go up. You find a grower willing to sell at eight cents, and (to keep this in round numbers) you tell him you will take ten lots of his 1975 crop. A lot is fifty-six tons, so ten lots will be 1,120,000 pounds of sugar, which at eight cents a pound means that you now owe the grower $99,600. But you have to put up only 10 percent of this, or $9960. For less than $10,000, which is to say for less than the cost of a luxury automobile, you now have acquired title to 1,120,000 pounds of sugar.

Not that you actually want the sugar. Heaven forbid! You don't even use the stuff in your coffee. You never want to see that sugar. At some time before the cane is cut, you want to sell your ten lots to a sugar trader or to some other bettor in the futures market. If the price should turn down, you will want to sell out as fast as you can before you take too much of a beating; if as you suppose, the price will go up, you stand to make a little money. You are not interested in sugar; you are interested in money.

For reasons as mysterious as those of the stock market, prices in the futures market slide up and down on guesses, on rumor, on what other plungers are willing to bet. In the fall of 1974, you can hardly believe your good fortune. The spot price on sugar now stands at forty-five cents. That is what someone is willing to pay for it, and the question in your mind is whether to sell, or to hang on, hoping the price will go even higher. Your decision is to sell. You sell your 1,120,000 pounds of future sugar at forty-five cents a pound, which amounts to $504,000. You have made a profit of thirty-seven cents a pound, or $414,400, on an original investment of $9960. You will have to pay a capital gains tax, but you can console yourself with the thought that if you had actually earned that much money, your tax would have been higher. Your essential contribution to your fellow man is that, by writing your name on a couple of checks, you have added half a million dollars to the price he will have to pay for sugar; you will have helped to increase the price of everything else in America, and particularly the price of food, and for your pains you wind up with at least $300,000 free and clear in the bank.

Well might all the rest of us ask, "Who needs you?"

Some of us might also wonder who needs a system that permits the existence of people like you. There will be a congressional investigation of the futures market. The congressmen know little about its workings at this time, so they are by no means prepared to say that all the workings of such a market are evil.

For example, there may be a real need and place for a

broker whose cash money down helps a grower set out his crop; who accepts delivery of the cut cane at his warehouse; who makes the sale to a refinery; who arranges for shipping space; who delivers the sugar cane to the refiner. Such a man has done more than risk his capital; he has also done some actual and necessary work.

The speculator is someone else again. He buys corn or wheat or sugar as if each were common stock certificates. But they are not stock certificates. They are products. The quoted market prices of corn, wheat, and sugar are the actual sales prices of those products. If their prices go up, then everyone who needs corn, wheat, and sugar will have to pay more for them. On the other hand, the prices of common stocks can rise and fall on the New York Stock Exchange without having the slightest effect on the retail prices of the products made by the companies whose stock is being traded. Not all of those products are actually necessary to human life. Speculators in the stock market can lose their shirts or make a fortune without loss or gain to anyone but themselves.

The congressmen who will look into the operation of the futures market do not believe the market itself is inherently ridiculous. They do, however, wonder if legislation might be required to make sure that no one can unfairly speculate within the market — particularly inasmuch as everyone in the nation is directly affected by such speculations.

As strangely as the sugar rocket had soared out of sight, it strangely reappeared, slowly descending. In the winter of 1974–75, the price of sugar began to fall. It must not be allowed to fall too fast, we were told by the writers of financial news — although why not was never made quite clear. One gathered that if sugar fell too fast the nation would collapse. Some people wondered why the refineries had not bought cheap Mexican sugar when the domestic price of cane and beets shot up. A few suspicious souls guessed that is exactly what they had done, but without telling anyone about it. It was all quite mysterious. In any event, the sugar rocket reappeared, slowly and majestically descending, and the great sugar shortage was over, if in fact there had ever been a shortage at all.

Hamburger à la Broad

The meat prices of 1974 were of concern to everyone in the nation; certainly to the cattlemen, who were facing bankruptcy because they were receiving less money for their steers than the cost of raising them; certainly to the housewives, who organized boycotts of supermarket meat counters to protest outrageous store prices. The high cost of meat was also a matter of concern to meat packers and supermarket managers, who complained to congressional committees of special problems in large cities. They did not spell out in detail just what those special problems were, nor did the congressmen question the witnesses closely about them.

Perhaps the special problems seemed too small or too local to warrant minute attention. I would disagree, not only because the existence of such problems has an effect upon the price we all pay for meat, but also because they illustrate a penalty we pay for living in large communities. Let us look for a moment into a special problem that afflicts the largest of our cities, and then we can decide whether it is a local problem.

There is in New York City a businessman named John Dioguardi, also known as Johnny Dio, and the word around New York is that if you refuse to do business with Johnny, he is very likely to give you the business. He is, according to police, a captain in the Luchese Family: in a word, a *Mafioso.*

Police observed him to be frequently in the company of

Moe Steinman, who is, or was, the director of labor relations for a New York City supermarket chain.

In 1974, Mr. Steinman pleaded guilty to one count of income tax evasion, a bit of naughtiness punishable by five years in a cage and a $10,000 fine. Mr. Steinman was told, however, that the judge was a lover of music and that if Mr. Steinman should burst into song, the judge might take a lenient view of Mr. Steinman's felonious behavior and not subject him to the full rigor of the law.

Specifically, Mr. Steinman was advised to sing a little aria about his having conspired with three officials of a butchers' union, executives of nine major supermarket chains, meat wholesalers, supermarket buying agents, and officials of Iowa Beef, Inc., of Dakota City, Nebraska. Iowa Beef is the world's largest beef-processing corporation, a going concern that does one and a half billion dollars' worth of business a year. Any grace notes Mr. Steinman might want to add about Johnny Dio would of course be music to the court's ears, but no one expected Mr. Steinman to be so foolish as to add them.

Mr. Steinman might never have found himself in court if Iowa Beef had not invented a box. The company believed that if a beef carcass could be cut up at the plant and specially wrapped and shipped in a 400-pound box, it would be more welcome at a supermarket than an unbutchered carcass would be — because Iowa Beef could cut up an animal more cheaply than supermarket butchers could and because boxed beef could be shipped more cheaply than whole carcasses. The supermarket's savings in labor costs and shipping charges could be passed on to the consumer, if the supermarket wished to do a thing like that. Iowa Beef figured the savings to the consumer would work out at five cents a pound. As Iowa Beef expected, the supermarkets were delighted to buy boxed beef.

The Amalgamated Meat Cutters and Butcher Workmen

(AFL-CIO) were not equally enchanted. Their spokesman, Arnold Mayer, admitted there were savings to be made by the packers and the markets, but he said the consumer would never see them. As far as the consumer was concerned, he said, the price of the special wrapping and boxing *added* five cents a pound to the cost of the beef, and that was more than the entire labor cost of slaughtering and processing the animal.

In St. Louis, Chicago, and New York City, union butchers in supermarkets saw boxed beef as a threat to their jobs. It appeared that if Iowa Beef was going to get its boxed beef to market, it would be only by labor's consent. The man to see about this in New York, the company learned, was Moe Steinman. According to testimony given by Iowa Beef officials to prosecuting attorneys and to the court, the company expected Mr. Steinman to be a crook:

"The reputation of New York City preceded our involvement with . . . Moe Steinman, and the opinion that we had of New York City was bad. We felt that it was a common practice that people paid other people off to do business in New York City . . . Anybody that's in the meat business in New York City is a crook."

The thought that if one engages in a criminal transaction one might become party to a criminal act apparently never crossed the corporate mind of Iowa Beef. It did, however, enter the minds of district attorneys, who accused Iowa Beef of agreeing to pay Mr. Steinman a commission of twenty-five cents on every hundred pounds of beef sold in all the supermarkets within a 125-mile radius of Columbus Circle in New York City.

Five dollars a ton for Mr. Steinman. And how many hundreds of thousands of tons of beef are annually consumed by the millions and millions of people who live within 125 miles of Columbus Circle?

And what valuable services would Mr. Steinman perform

to earn this princely fee? The prosecution's general field theory of labor relativity in this case goes thus: Mr. Steinman would make the union officials an offer they couldn't refuse. They could either accept money to forget all about their union's objections to boxed beef and keep their rank and file in line, or else. The implication was that Johnny Dio was also known as Else.

The money was paid, the prosecution said, and no picket lines appeared, and Iowa Beef's boxed beef came to the richest marketplace in the world. But then, the prosecution said, Mr. Steinman told the vice-president and treasurer of Iowa Beef that the price had just gone up. From now on, Mr. Steinman would want fifty cents on every hundred pounds, or ten bucks a ton, and when the startled corporate official wondered why, Mr. Steinman explained, as though to a child:

"Well, kid, I have other expenses, too. There are three kinds. I pay meat buyers off at fifteen percent; I pay union people at seven percent; and it costs me ten percent to convert the corporate money to cash, and I have to deal in cash. I've got to buy a union steward . . . I've got to buy a guy a broad; I may have to buy a chain-store buyer; and I've got to pay in cash."

Police could readily imagine Mr. Steinman's need of cash, and also his need of washing the checks, and they supposed he patronized his friendly neighborhood Mafia self-service laundry.

How interesting it is to know that if you eat a hamburger within 125 miles of Columbus Circle, part of the money you pay helps a pimp to fix a guy up with a broad — but maybe that is why they call New York Fun City.

How interesting it is, too, to reflect that a billion-dollar corporation might truckle to a crook; to think that it would actually *expect* to do so as a matter of routine business practice. Is organized crime in New York City mightier than a billion dollars? One might think that if Iowa Beef wished to buy a social service, it would think in terms of buying the services of the cops rather than those of the robbers.

The questions raised in this case are much more important than the specific fates of Mr. Steinman and the fates of those with whom he may have conspired. Here we have crooked middlemen preying on middlemen in the food chain, ultimately extorting money from everyone who buys beef within 125 miles of our principal city — a not insignificant segment of the national populace.

They are able to do this, I think, only because of the impersonality of the multitude. It is difficult to imagine anything of the sort taking place in a village, where everyone would know all there is to know about everyone else, and where anyone who tried to extort money from others might reasonably expect to find himself sitting in the stocks on the village green, or suddenly leaving town on a rail, wearing a costume of hot roofing tar and pullet feathers.

But New York is not a village. It is a large city that is becoming less governable every day. It is the living, or dying, proof that an impersonal society is inimical to the quality of human life, and I think that what is true of New York City in this regard is applicable to the nation as a whole.

The special problem of doing business in large cities, to which the meat packers and supermarket managers referred, is not local and has nothing really to do with the likes of Moe Steinman and Johnny Dio. The special problem that plagues the entire nation has to do with a system that deals in huge numbers. When food is massively produced and mass-marketed by anonymous corporations to masses of total strangers, no one person seems to be responsible for anything, decisions are made in terms of numbers, and the

numbers refer to dollars and cents and not to anything else
— least of all to people. Through no one's real fault, but
because almost everyone has been bemused by numbers, we
have arrived at an agricultural and marketing system that
supplies an enormous population with a diminished variety
of foodstuffs, of indifferent quality, at constantly escalating
prices, and that, if it is designed at all, is designed to produce
maximum profits while meeting the minimal needs of a
captive mass market of urban consumers. We have, as we
have seen, arrived at a situation in which the nutritional
value of food can be decreased while the price of the food is
increased; in which monopolies can be achieved; in which
speculators can find opportunities to make money without
performing the slightest service; in which gangsters can
discover alleys suitably dark for their purposes; and in which
one of the world's largest corporations deems it prudent to
do business with the gangsters. If, as once we did, we bought
our produce and our meats directly from farmers, or from
shopkeepers supplied by local farmers, the situation would
not exist. We eat what we do, and pay for it what we must,
because of the way we live, and it is the way we live that is
our special problem.

Price and Paranoia

"In the past sixty years," a U.S. Food and Drug Administration pamphlet says, "America has undergone a great agricultural and scientific revolution. Before that time the American food supply was largely processed and consumed on the
family farm. Now food is processed and packaged in giant
factories, bought at the supermarket, and consumed thousands of miles from where it was grown. Miracles of
transportation and technology have made this possible.

Advances in food . . . technology have provided a variety of
foods . . . our forefathers never knew — but they have also
created new problems. When people raised their own food
— or bought it from a neighbor — they had control over its
purity and quality. In modern times, however, no consumer
can exercise such control himself. Government must do for
all what no individual can do alone."

The problems to which the FDA referred are a source of
worry to a young woman named Barbara, who lives in
Pittsburgh with her two infants and a husband who cannot
abide Brussels sprouts. When Barbara goes to the store, it is
simple enough for her to remember not to buy Brussels
sprouts, but it is something else again to know what to buy
for her babies, because she recently read that prepared baby
foods "often contain unnecessary ingredients such as sugar
and starch, as well as salt, spices, and sodium nitrite . . . a
preservative . . . suspected of being a potential source of
cancer."

Barbara had never before heard of the Center for Science
in the Public Interest of Washington, D.C., which was the
source of the quotation that appeared in her local newspaper,
and she knew that the word "often" means "not usually,"
and she was aware that saying "suspected of being a
potential cause" is a very different thing from saying "*is* a
cause." Nevertheless, what she read disturbed her.

"Why take a chance with your baby's life?" she asked.

"If you feel that way, then stay away from baby foods,"
her husband, who is a physician, told her.

"It's not feeling," she told him. "Who's talking about
feeling? I'm talking about knowing. I want to know. Is
baby food bad for babies or not?"

Her husband had too much respect for his science to
venture an opinion in a field about which he knew nothing.
He knew, for example, that too much salt can be bad for

some people; for that matter, that too much of anything can be bad for anyone. But he lacked the data that might have led him to form an opinion as to whether X baby food might prove harmful to his babies. He doubted that any of the baby foods were harmful, but that was just a doubt, not something he knew to be a fact. There was something he could do, however, to put his wife's fears to rest.

"Don't buy them," he told her. He said it *was* a fact that after a child is weaned it can eat whatever its parents eat, providing that the food is ground or mashed. Millions of babies have grown to maturity for thousands of years without the assistance of the baby food industry, he pointed out. In many lands, millions of babies still do. All Barbara needed was a chopping knife and a potato masher, if not a cheap food grinder or even an expensive electric blender. Then her problems would be over. They would save money into the bargain, he said, because it stood to reason that processed baby foods were more expensive than foods prepared at home. After all, when you buy a jar of baby food, you pay for the jar, the cap, the label, and the cost of a corporation's doing a profitable business, as well as for the food in the jar. Prepared baby foods were therefore unnecessary in the first place, expensive in the second, and their sole value lay in their convenience.

Barbara was thankful for this advice, but she was still not quite clear of the nutritional woods, because if she was going to make a purée for her babies out of what she and her husband normally ate, her next problem was to be sure that what *they* ate was healthful.

"I stay away from *all* prepared foods," Barbara told me, "because it is not only the salt, but it's the sugar they have in them, and, my God! the chemicals! I don't want to sound as if I'm a health nut or anything; I don't really think I am. But do you have any idea how many chemicals they put in, and nobody knows what they do to you?"

She produced a copy of *The Poisons in Your Food** and opened it to the section wherein author William Longwood said, "Virtually every bite of food you eat has been treated with some chemical somewhere along the line," and went on to parade an ominous-sounding list of them. "These," he wrote, "are the tools of the food technician . . . His alchemy can make stale products appear fresh, permit unsanitary practices, mask inferior quality, substitute nutritionally inferior or worthless chemicals for more costly natural ingredients. These chemicals, almost without exception, perform their mission at the cost of destroying valuable vitamins, minerals and enzymes, stripping food products of their natural life-giving qualities."

"When I go to the store, I want to buy only fresh foods," Barbara said, "and only fresh meats. I don't buy bacon, ham, or sausages, not because I'm religious or because I don't like them, but because they have chemicals in them that might give some people cancer, and nobody knows whether they do or not, but who needs cancer? When I buy fresh fruits and vegetables, I have to scrub or peel them to make sure I get off whatever somebody might have sprayed on them, and even then who knows what might have got into them when they were growing, with all the fertilizers and pesticides they use now?

"Look," she said, "I don't like to sound as if I'm scared to death every time I go to the store — I really don't think I am — but I mean that going to the store isn't really a whole lot of fun. When I go to the store, I want to buy food, not a lot of chemicals. I don't think that's too much to ask, do you? I like food, I really do, but they're taking all the fun out of it."

To use her own description of herself, Barbara is not a health nut or anything. She is an intelligent woman who would like to know exactly what she is buying when she goes

* Pyramid Books, New York, 1969.

into the supermarket, and there are a great many other people who would like to know, too. It is perfectly true that almost every food sold has been subjected to some sort of processing by middlemen, and it is also true that some of the processes diminish the nutritive content of the treated food and that others may render a food positively harmful to some people. There has been such a flood of warnings, charges, countercharges, and criticism of the food industry that Dr. Jean Mayer has said it all sounds like a quarrel of paranoiacs to him — implying that our food supply is not really as poisonous as some critics say it is, nor quite so wonderful as spokesmen for the food industry would have it appear.

The ever multiplying quantities of convenience foods, or fastfoods, are a major source of concern. Apart from whatever may have been done to bring to market the fresh foods you would normally prepare in the kitchen, such as the immature tomatoes that have been gassed to make them appear to be ripe, there are literally thousands of foodstuffs upon our grocery shelves that are entirely the confections of the food factories to which the FDA pamphlet referred. These include foodstuffs that have already been cooked, such as frozen TV dinners and all sorts of canned foods and canned dinners that need only to be thawed or heated to be served. There are cake mixes, dehydrated fruits, dehydrated vegetables, and meats that need only to be mixed with water. Prepared doughs turn themselves into breads and rolls when you turn on the oven. There are all manner of instant foods, including breakfast cereals, crackers, synthetic cheeses, cocktail snacks, cereals, pies, and beverages that need only to be unwrapped to be eaten or drunk. These convenience foods, or fastfoods, are seen by some nutritionists to be a primary reason for the nation's generally poor health. The American Medical Association, in its book *Let's Talk About Food*, doubts that "industrially created foods" are capable of "maintaining life and energy" among the people who eat them. Temple University's Health Service Center reports that cooked or processed foodstuffs often lose some of their natural value in preparation; that prolonged storage on a grocery shelf can decrease, if not absolutely deplete, the value of the food in the box; and that some fastfoods, which contain only carbohydrates, fat, and additives that make them look, smell, and taste delicious, are not really food at all because they contain no proteins, vitamins, or minerals. Frozen orange concentrate does not have quite the same nutritive quality that fresh orange juice has, the FDA says, adding that nutritional values break down slightly whenever a food is frozen and thawed — and that there is no way the shopper can know how many times a package of frozen food may have been inadvertently thawed and then refrozen during all the handling it receives between the moment it leaves the factory and the time someone puts it into the supermarket's frozen-food chest.

Quotations and citations could be multiplied, but only to make the point that a problem does exist, whether it sends some people into paranoia or not. The United States government is concerned about it, but not to the point of prohibiting the manufacture of convenience foods or even of junk foods. The government's position is interesting. Much as the FDA might say that government must do for all what no individual can do alone, the FDA by no means seeks to save the people from themselves. Indeed, it regards the convenience food industry as one that is merely responding to public demand.

"There are thirty-one million working women," an FDA official, Bob Lockett, said, "so naturally there's a market for instant potatoes, frozen vegetables that cook in ten minutes, TV dinners, canned soups, and so on. In America, you give the public what it demands."

This point of view, general in the FDA, may be a

somewhat short sale of working women, who spend exactly as much time in the kitchen as do women who do not work outside the house, and an even shorter sale of the inventiveness of the food industry. For example, it is most unlikely that overwhelming multitudes of working women got down on their knees in the front of the Durkee Food Service Group's Cleveland offices and begged for a "total tomato replacement."

In describing this contribution to our larder, a Durkee advertisement in a food industry journal says, "There is no acid taste or color loss, and just two ounces of the concentrate approximates the flavor and aroma of thirty bushels of fresh tomatoes . . . The new product contains potato and wheat flours, dextrose, salt, sugar, artificial and natural flavors, propylene glycol alginate, certified food colors, and up to 2% of silicon dioxide as an anti-caking agent. The product can then be used as a one-for-one direct replacement for natural tomato."

Instead of believing that the public demanded a cheap chemical substitute for real tomatoes, it is easier to imagine that the Durkee Group figured it could market such a product if it made one, thereby undercutting the market in real tomatoes, and that any housewife who in the future bought something called Mama Mia's Real Red Clam Sauce would never know there were no tomatoes in it, or would really care if she knew there were none, or had any idea what "real" Italian cooking was, just so long as whatever it was tasted all right.

The FDA believes that, in meeting the public's demands, the food industry should not poison the public. But this is a point of view that sometimes falls well short of restraint, as in the matter of vitamin pills. The FDA printed a pamphlet called *Myths of Vitamins*, which, in brief, warned that overdoses of vitamins can do mental and physical damage to infants and actually kill people; that the only people who should ever take vitamin pills are those medical patients who have been found to suffer from a specific vitamin deficiency and who are given the appropriate pills by a licensed physician. Otherwise, the pamphlet said, a balanced diet gives anyone all the vitamins anyone needs. Any advertisement showing someone taking vitamin pills "just to be sure" is nothing in the world but a dangerous lie. "The simplest, surest guide to follow for a good daily balance of nutrients," the FDA said, "is still the selection of foods from each of four larger groups: milk, meat, vegetable/fruit, and bread/cereal."

It was Barbara, by the way, who came across this pamphlet, and when she showed it to her doctor-husband, he said that what the pamphlet said was true.

"If that's so," she almost shouted, "why do they let anybody sell them? The stores are full of vitamin pills! Why doesn't the FDA stop it?"

To her it was simple enough: Big Brother knows a substance is dangerous. But Big Brother allows it to be sold. Then, in an obscure pamphlet that most people will never see or even hear about, Big Brother says, for God's sake, don't buy it; it is unnecessary at best and lethal at worst. And if *that* is Big Brother's idea of saving us all from a clutch of industrial Borgias, we might as well forget about the government and start looking out for ourselves.

Actually, Big Brother is just as badly beset as we are and is as much in need of our help as we are of his. When in 1906 the administration proposed a Pure Food and Drug Act, all suggested standards relative to food were withdrawn from it at the behest of lawyers representing the nation's whiskey blenders.

When in 1938 a federal Food, Drug and Cosmetic Act was passed, it did put an end to some of the less imaginative forms of cheating. No longer could a manufacturer bottle a colorful goo made of glucose and hayseed and sell it as "raspberry jam." The act was full of loopholes, however, and all during the subsequent decades the FDA has been trying to close them. But as an FDA pamphlet says, "Insuring the integrity of food is a continuing problem. At the same time it has become increasingly difficult to establish new standards if there is opposition. Industry lawyers delayed final action on a peanut butter standard for over ten years . . . Strong, well-informed consumer support is a necessity in the standard-making procedure."

But who is to inform the consumer so that he can support the FDA? For example, in 1973 a San Francisco physician suspected that some artificial food flavors and colors used in the manufacture of multicolored breakfast cereals, potato chips, soda pops, and powdered drink mixes make some children hyperactive and impair their learning abilities. No one had ever imagined anything of the sort before, and when the doctor told the FDA of his suspicions, the agency was totally (and properly) skeptical — and the physician complained that the agency was not supporting *him.*

Today, two experiments are underway, one of them set up at FDA's urging, to test the San Francisco doctor's hypothesis. Until the case against the flavors and colors is proved, the additives will certainly be used — no matter that some of the children who ingest them *may* become hyperactive slow learners. Then, even if the experiments confirm the doctor's suspicions, this would not necessarily mean the FDA would *forthwith* ban the use of the harmful flavors and colors, although that would certainly be one possibility.

Instead, the FDA might remember that the junk food and bellywash industries represent no small part of the national economy, and that to order them summarily to stop using those flavors and colors would be to precipitate a multimillion-dollar catastrophe and add whole battalions of workers to the army of the unemployed. In that case, the FDA might very well permit the junk food industry to continue to use the harmful additives for a limited time, during which the industry would be enjoined to find flavorings and colors that would not do damage to children. Meanwhile, the packages and bottles of brightly colored junk and bellywash would have to carry labels.

HYPERKINETICS — The Surgeon General wants you to know he does not believe what you are about to ingest may be entirely without certain potentially deleterious consequences, including exacerbation, consternation, and exegesis, owing to concentrations of polysyllabic manbanes including diobasis, anabasis, cryptostaticpodosporyluminate, and ethylazosiaminide.

Thus, every little seven-year-old who had a medical degree or a competent knowledge of biochemistry, and who had no trouble spelling would be duly warned, so that if he went ahead and bought the stuff anyway, that would be his fault, wouldn't it.

Rather similar decisions have been made in the recent past. A case in which the FDA allowed the use of a potential carcinogen, in order not to do catastrophic damage to an industry, involved a red dye derived from a coal tar. The dye had been used for years to make oranges orange. Since most Americans have never seen oranges growing, they do not know that ripe oranges are not necessarily orange. But since the public had been led to believe that oranges are orange when ripe, America's citrus growers obligingly dyed them, and used the coal tar dye to do so. Of course the growers did not know that the dye could cause cancer — and for many years, no one else did, either. When the fact was at last discovered, the FDA and the citrus industry had a problem. Not to dye the oranges would be the same thing as not to sell them, for the public would reject oranges that were not orange. The public could have been educated from its erroneous belief by massive government and industry publicity, but it was felt that this would take time, and during that time the citrus industry might well be ruined. The FDA resolved the matter by permitting the growers to continue using the dye for a time long enough to permit them to find another dye that was demonstrably harmless. In so doing, the agency invoked a measurement of its own, called "the risk/benefit formula."

Briefly, this means the public assumes the risk and the food industry benefits. If there is some faint risk that some people might in some circumstances be poisoned by a chemical additive suspected, but not proved, to be harmful to people, and if this chemical's use is absolutely essential in getting a valuable food to market, then the chances are excellent that the FDA will pass that faint risk on to us, and rule in favor of the food industry.

Such was the case with respect to oranges, and such is the case with respect to the nitrates and nitrites used to preserve ham, bacon, hot dogs and other processed meats, and some smoked fish. The chemical additives fix the color; that is, they prevent red meat from turning brown, and they also prevent deadly botulism organisms from forming in the meat. Some people have a body chemistry that converts nitrites into nitrosamines, and nitrosamines can cause cancer. In considering this risk, the FDA had to take into account the fact that for hundreds of years people have been using those chemicals to preserve pork products; to reflect that the chemicals were certainly protective against botulism; to weigh the importance of those chemicals to the hugely powerful and politically important meat processing industry

— and put all this against what it called "the unknown risk" that these otherwise beneficial chemicals "may" form a compound in your gut that "could" cause you to die in agony. Interestingly enough, the FDA implies that the risk is very real. "Any change in the regulation of these additives," an FDA spokesman said, "must await the results of the research now underway."

The FDA's problems are indeed manifold. Research cannot keep pace with invention. Whenever the FDA proposes a regulation, twenty-eight bright lawyers, hired by the food industry, discover four hundred and sixty-nine clever reasons for opposing it or ways of skating around it. The agency is subject to political pressure insofar as it receives its money and its orders from Congress, and insofar as congressmen will listen to the sound of big money speaking through the plausible suggestions of lobbyists.

Money is what food additives are really all about. Some are beneficial in rendering food germ-free. Some add nutrients to synthetic foods that would otherwise be a pile of glop. Some render foods rancid-proof, thereby enabling the food to be transported over vast distances and held for long periods of time in warehouses or on store shelves. Other additives do nothing for foodstuffs except make them salable. They add no nutrient value, but give processed foods color, flavor, and that texture the food industry technicians call "mouthfeel." Additives also make possible the concoction of wholly new food products, confected in chemical laboratories from such unlikely bases as yeasts grown on piles of garbage.

All additives cost money, and they all add up to money. No food processor would add a penny's worth of any of them to any food whatsoever if he did not believe he could make money by doing this. They are not added by the pennyworth. One estimate is that the food industry uses half a billion dollars' worth of additives every year, and feeds five pounds of them to each of us every year even if we might not want them. Additives add cost. John M. Volkhardt, president of the Best Foods division of Corn Products Company International, Inc., said that the more any food product is tinkered with, gussied up, or otherwise processed, the less its retail price has to do with the farm price of the natural food it contains, and the less likely its price is ever to come down at the supermarket. Without additives, the current American system of producing, processing, and marketing foodstuffs could not exist, and this is entirely and particularly true of the convenience, or fastfood, industry, where a chief purpose of using additives is the creation of illusions.

Durkee's "total tomato replacement" is an illusion of tomatoes.

"The key to great meat products is great meat flavor," said an advertisement addressed to meat processors by H. Kohnstamm and Company of New York, Chicago, and Los Angeles. "That's why you select the choicest cuts of meat, because they have the most flavor potential. But too often that flavor gets lost through processing or quick freezing. So after processing, your product may need a boost to recapture its flavor potential. Kohnstamm meat flavors are natural-tasting. So they can restore the mouth-watering essence of prime meat, freshly cut from the butcher's block, then cooked to perfection. Rejuvenate your meat products with Kohnstamm chicken, beef, turkey, ham, bacon or other meat flavors. We'll not only supply the flavor, we'll help you fit it into your base . . . Now's the time to come back to natural-tasting meat flavor. Call us today or write for more information."

Hercules, Inc., well aware how awful synthetic or processed foods can taste, advertises that "our cellulose gums and carrageenans [a seeweed] are widely used to stabilize, thicken and bind; add body and improve mouthfeel . . . If you're in the business of making and marketing convenience food, we're in the business of helping you make it better. In taste, in texture, in mouthfeel." [But not in nutritive value.]

Insofar as the food industry does not talk about illusion, it talks about money. "We think," Chemetron Corporation told meat processors, "in terms of your profitable end results, rather than in terms of traditionally accepted processing steps and procedures." But most of the talk is about illusion, and herein, I think, lies the true danger of additives. It is not so much that some additives make foods more expensive than they would otherwise be, or that they threaten to poison us all, although we are all aware of the price of food these days, and although a fear of poisoning has induced a degree of paranoia in otherwise competent people like Barbara.

Surely an ability to discriminate between the real and the unreal is at least one indication of mental health. Another indication of a sound mind is a person's willingness to be guided by, and to act upon, what he knows to be true. The truly deleterious effect of the convenience food industry is to blur distinction, to substitute approximation or illusion for reality, and to offer an excuse for choosing the false instead of the real.

For example, real ice cream is made out of cream, sugar, a natural flavor (such as that derived from using real strawberries), and, perhaps, eggs. Additives enable a manufacturer to combine dried skim milk, corn syrup, artificial strawberry flavor, and seaweed into something he can sell as "strawberry ice cream." Of course this concoction is not really ice cream, any more than the "real mayonnaise" sold in jars in supermarkets is really mayonnaise. Really real mayonnaise is made by beating dry mustard, salt, pepper, lemon juice, and a bit of sugar into beaten egg yolks and slowly drizzling olive oil into the mixture while continuing to beat it with a whisk, and adding a few more drops of lemon juice and vinegar. Whatever herbs you might add are optional. How real the store's "real mayonnaise" may be can be deduced from the label. "Ingredients," the label says: "Vegetable salad oil, whole eggs, vinegar, water, egg yolks, salt, sugar, lemon juice and natural flavors. Calcium diosodium EDTA added to protect flavor."

The ingredients of real ice cream and real mayonnaise are more expensive than the store substitutes. To make ice cream at home is a tedious process, often requiring the services of children whose reward is licking the paddles, and making mayonnaise is also a somewhat arduous process that takes time and, sometimes, four hands. But you wind up with real ice cream and with real mayonnaise, and the richness, color, taste, and texture of these foods is several light years distant from the light, pallid goos that are sold as "ice cream" and "real mayonnaise" in the supermarket. You cannot say that the store products are convenient and saving of time and labor unless you are willing to face the fact that you have chosen the false for the true, and that you have done this because you were unwilling to spend the money, time, and effort to acquire something genuine and settled instead for a cheap, illusory approximation of reality. If you are aware of this difference, then the store names of the products will be as insulting to your intelligence as their taste will be to your palate, and you may be left with a vague feeling of disappointment, if not one of guilty unease.

Of course it can be argued that almost no one wants to take the time and effort to make real ice cream and real mayonnaise every time he wants them, but to say this is to say that we get exactly what we deserve.

Throughout the range of covenience foods, including such things as a packet of frozen beans or a box of cake mix, the rule is: *Less is here than meets the eye.*

Even the convenience is illusory.

For example, one thing said for frozen beans is that their preparation is simplicity itself. You pop them into boiling water, and a few minutes later they are done. Is that so?

Let us say you have a choice at the store. There is a bin of fresh green beans, maybe not the best you've ever seen, but certainly as fresh and crisp as ever they are at the store. Then there are packages of frozen beans in the frozen-food locker. You choose the frozen ones and cook them for supper.

This actually means that you take a pot from its place in the kitchen, put water and salt into it, put it on the stove, turn on the burner, open the refrigerator, take the package of green beans from the freezer compartment, close the refrigerator door, open the package, wait for the water to boil, put the beans into it, and await future developments. You throw away the package. Later, you remove the beans from the water, strain them, put them into a serving dish, season them with nutmeg if you wish, and carry the dish to the table. After supper, you wash and dry the pot and the strainer and return them to their places in the kitchen.

Where is the convenience? All you have really saved yourself is the few minutes' difference between opening a package and breaking up a few fresh beans. You could have broken the beans while the water was coming to a boil. Otherwise, you use just as many utensils to cook fresh beans as frozen ones; you go through the same cooking procedure; and the cooking time is, or should be, the same. (I am aware that some people boil fresh beans for twenty minutes, but they may not be aware that to do so is to cook out most of the nutrients.) The fresh beans are slightly more nutritious than the frozen ones, tastier, and less expensive. The true convenience of frozen foods is the convenience to the food processor: he can buy up beans by the ton when their price hits rock bottom and sell them all year long at a uniformly high price.

As in the case of frozen foods, the supposed advantage of the cake mix is that it saves you time. But whether you bake from a mix or from scratch, you must trot out the utensils and the bowls, grease the baking pan, mix the batter, turn on the oven, pour the batter into the baking pan, put the pan in the oven, clean up the bowls and utensils, put them away, take the pan out of the oven when the cake is done, put the cake on a plate, and clean the baking pan. It takes only a few moments longer to assemble for yourself the ingredients the cake mix contains, and if you bake from scratch, you have absolute quality control over those ingredients, which you do not have over the ingredients in the mix. More important, you have baked your own cake, and not, let us say, Betty Crocker's idea of one, and you may therefore take a proper pride in real accomplishment. Furthermore, it is twice as expensive to use a mix as it is to bake from scratch. Again, the real convenience of the cake mix is its convenience to the manufacturer.

My experience is that any time saved in the kitchen is more apt to be saved by machines than by frozen foods or mixes. If I am going to make a sauce for meat, and if this involves mincing onions, carrots, celery, and parsley, I can spend almost half an hour chopping away with a knife, or about two minutes using an electric blender. The same can be said for beating batter with a spoon or using an electric mixer. But it would seem that all talk about convenience foods' saving time in the kitchen is the discussion of an illusion.

If there is any convenience food that really saves time, that would be the frozen dinner. Unfortunately, however, only too many of them also save you from ingesting much of anything that could honestly be called food; the frozen dinner is the particular bête noir of the nutritionist.

The existence of all the middlemen who compose the packing, processing, convenience, fastfood, junk food, and bellywash industries is a function of distances. These include our distance from the land and a knowledge thereof, the distance in time from when a food is garnered until it is eaten, the physical distances our foods travel from farm to supermarkets, the distances between processed and fresh foodstuffs, and the distance between illusion and reality.

It is the latter distance on which these middlemen have particularly capitalized, almost as if they consciously understood and deliberately acted on America's willingness to accept the similar for the genuine, America's belief that something new must therefore be somehow better, America's age-long love affair with anything that seems to promise a saving of money, time, and effort. Their advertising rings constant changes upon such bells.

VIDEO	AUDIO
Sunlight left rear. Four white, one black, eight-year-old boys; baseball caps, bat, gloves. At kitchen table. Young white mother pours the Product in bowls as	*Announcer (voice over)* "Mothers! It's New! It's Here! Crunchy! Nourishing! Goodness — Like wheat! Golden flakes give instant energy!
Kids clap, laugh, reach.	"How they love it!
Close on Product. Hold Glory Shot.	"Yes! All New! New Yocko Whockos! Crunchy! Husky! Golden like wheat!"
Pull back, show kids gobbling. Close on fat white kid, freckles, rubber face.	*Fat Kid* "Yocko Whockos make me strong."

Long view. Mother smiling. Close on Young Mother. She listens as Announcer gives the Message. Close on Product.	*Announcer (voice over)* "Yocko Whockos make kids strong! Doctors say one bowl gives energy today's children need! Yocko Whockos — Golden, like wheat! At your store today!
Hold Glory Shot.	"Makes kids strong!"
Back to table. Kids scrape bowls. Fat Kid licks spoon.	*Fat Kid* "I bet I hit a million home runs!"

The cost of this advertisement is present in every box of Yocko Whockos. Specifically, every time you spend a dollar for dry breakfast cereal, you pay thirty-three cents of it for the privilege of being misled, told at least one half-truth and three outright lies. Thirty-three percent of the package price is the average cost of advertising purchased by the nation's four major cereal firms, who manufacture eighty percent of all the dry breakfast cereals you see in the store and who make ninety-one percent of the cereal trade profit. You also pay for the box, and the cost of the box is far greater than the cost of the cereal it contains. You pay for the costs of cutting, puffing, or otherwise shaping the grain. The reason for this puffing and shaping is to make it appear that one box contains a different product from that of another when such is not the case. You now pay part of your money for something you can actually eat: artificial coloring, artificial flavoring, chemical preservatives, and sugar. None of these additives possesses nutritional value. No less than fifty percent of the net weight of one dry breakfast cereal is the weight of the sugar with which it is coated. Sugar nourishes no one. Its presence in the package is simply explained: it is there to serve as child-bait. Next, you pay some of your money for something that is good for you; namely, the synthetic nutrients and synthetic vitamins that have been added to restore to the grain some of the nutritional value that processing had taken out of it. The last and least part of your dollar buys a bit of grain. To put the matter as kindly as possible, the Yocko Whocko industry lies expensively to little children and sells a product that is ridiculous to the point of utter absurdity when compared, bowlful to bowlful, with much cheaper cooked whole grain.

Two government agencies, the Federal Trade Commission and the Food and Drug Administration, do what they can to control what food processors claim in their advertisements and put on their labels. Both the reason for their concern and the extent of their concern were nicely summed up by an FDA official.

"Today's housewife," he said, "must become a label reader, because she can't survive otherwise. I mean, survive economically and nutritionally. Unless she reads the labels, she can pay too much and get too little."

New advertising and labeling regulations, promulgated in 1974 and 1975, represent a small but historic shift in the government's basic philosophy of commerce. Heretofore, the government view had been "Let the buyer beware." The buyer was supposed to have a competent knowledge of foodstuffs, an intelligent command of English, and a lively suspicion of anyone who sold anything.

But the advent of chemically prepared foods, together with an agricultural innocence on the part of an urban population, the sound of alarm bells ringing in research laboratories, the swift rise in food prices, the weasel phrases of advertising, the pressures of specially informed groups acting in the consumer's interest all conspired to change the government's mind. The new regulations are in the direction of protecting the consumer from the hands of those who feed him. The emergent motto is "Let the seller beware."

New labels require the manufacturers of processed foods to make a complete disclosure of the contents. Yet much is still left to the public's informed discretion.

For example, you now see RDA labels on processed foods. RDA means Recommended Daily Allowance. You are supposed to know that the person for whom the allowance is recommended is a 154-pound American male in perfect health who is engaged in light work. Such a fellow, according to the National Academy of Sciences, should receive 2800 calories a day, and his diet should include 100 percent of the Recommended Daily Allowance of proteins, vitamins, and minerals. You are also supposed to know the difference between useful proteins and inutile ones, as well as knowing the entire table of vitamins and the roster of necessary minerals. You are also expected to have a competent knowledge of the following words: carbohydrate, sodium, fat, polyunsaturated, saturated, cholesterol, thiamine, niacin, riboflavin, and a knowledge of all the chemicals that may be listed in the statement of ingredients. For some shoppers, a chemistry textbook and a copy of *Merck's Manual* of advice to physicians could be helpful at this point. Now then, of course you know that the protein/calorie relationship ought to be 1:60. Please bear in mind that there are 454 grams to the pound, that 1 gram equals 1000 milligrams and that 1 milligram equals 1000 micrograms, and that 1 ounce equals 28 grams. Well, that works out to 448 grams a pound, doesn't it. But the conversion used by the government is approximate. Anyway, you will be all right if you use the rule of thumb — 450 grams to the pound — and you had better keep this in mind because when you read the RDA label it may say, "Serving size: 1 oz., Protein, 2g."

You are now ready to read the label, and you see "Serving size, 8 oz. Protein 23g. USRDA Protein, 35%." This means that if a 154-pound American male, who was in perfect health and did light work, ate a pound of this stuff, he would receive 46 grams of protein, which sounds like a lot until you remember that the "USRDA Protein" means *useful* protein, which means that 65 percent of each 23 grams of protein in this particular can of food is *not* useful. Very well, you will have to buy some additional foodstuffs to arrive at 100 percent of the RDA of useful protein; but meanwhile, have an eye to those calories, let's keep the ratio at 1:60, and remember all the time to be sure that what you buy also adds up to 100 percent of the RDA for all the vitamins and minerals needed by a 154-pound American male in perfect health who does light work.

If there is no such person in your family, you simply transpose all the figures to suit the daily requirements of your 250-pound husband who does heavy work and of your underweight daughter who does no work at all; and remember that your mother-in-law must watch her salt intake and that she is coming to dinner tonight.

Having all this in mind or worked out on your pocket calculator, you are now ready to buy wisely — which brings up the matter of money. Here are two packages of frozen creamed spinach. Both are offered at the same price, or at a price so close as to make no never-minds. One says "Serves four." The other says "Serves six." The new label requirements demand that the manufacturer level with you about this. Just as you are about to buy the package that promises to serve six for the price of feeding four, you remember to check the net weights. Both packages are twelve ounces. This leads you to read the rest of the information on the labels. The package that says "Serves four" says "Serving size, 3 oz." The other one says "Serving size, 2 oz."

You now begin to see why the FDA proudly says, "Nutrition information panels provide an easy way for consumers to learn about the nutritional value of food . . .

In addition, newly introduced foods can be compared with familiar ones to learn whether they are good nutritional buys."

If you do not think the labels add ease to your shopping, you must admit they are a step in the direction of consumer protection. There is meanwhile a simple alternative to label-reading: Stay away from *all* prepared foods. Just eat three meals a day of foods that, in sum, include fresh dairy products, meat or fish, vegetables including leafy ones, fruit, real bread and cereals. That should give you all the proteins, vitamins, minerals, and calories you need. If you are too skinny, eat more; if too fat, eat less. In any case, take regular exercise.

When you move on to the fresh-food counters, however, it is well to remember that some United States government labels can be as misleading as some of the manufacturers' advertising. Grade A on a milk label does NOT mean it is either tasty or nutritious. It simply means the milk has met government standards for production and processing. Similarly, Grade A on fruits and vegetables does NOT mean they will be either good to eat or good for you to eat; it means merely that they have met Department of Agriculture standards of *appearance*. Nor does the word "Choice" on beef necessarily mean what it used to mean. Late in 1974, with grain prices high and meat prices so low that cattlemen faced bankruptcy, the Department of Agriculture proposed to grant to grass-fed cattle the "Choice" label heretofore reserved for grain-fattened cattle. "All we can do," said a spokesman for the National Livestock and Meat Board, "is hope that the stores handle it with honesty and don't try to pass off this beef as something it isn't, or attach a meaningless name to it. Ideally, the term 'grass-fed' should appear somewhere on the package and the price should be lower. But that's ideally."

The entire thrust of the government's current concern for labeling is, however, toward honesty. Gone are the days of the "jumbo quart" and "giant pound," although manufacturers are still fighting a desultory rear-guard action with respect to "nonfunctional slack fill." The phrase refers to the space between the top of the product in the box and the top of the box. Such a space is "non-functional" when it is unnecessary either with respect to the integrity of the package itself or to the protection of the product in the package — but serves only the function of leading the customer to believe there is more in the box than there actually is. So far, the courts have taken the manufacturers' side in this, professing to see nothing wrong as long as the label accurately declares the quantity of the contents.

Containers of packaged nuts must now be at least 85 percent filled. If a package of mixed nuts contains one kind of nut whose weight exceeds the weight of the sum of all the others, the label must state the percentage of the predominant nut; that is, "contains 80 percent peanuts." No nut ingredient may be less than 2 percent or more than 80 percent. Any mix must contain at least four kinds of nuts, to which a fifth, peanuts, may be added. If the peanuts have skins on them, the label must say so unless there is a picture of unblanched peanuts on the package. All nut and non-nut ingredients must be declared on the label in the descending order of predominance, and any pictorial representation of the nuts must fairly reflect the appearance of the contents.

With respect to TV dinners, the requirement is a bit different. The picture on the package must "reasonably" resemble the appearance of the contents, and the weasel words accompanying the picture are "Serving suggestion." These words usually mean that the contents by no means resemble the picture unless you rearrange them so that they do. For example, the picture on a package of a frozen shrimp dinner may show a pile of pink, succulent shrimp in a sauce. It is "suggested" you serve them that way. The net weight of the contents will be marked on the package, and the ingredients are listed. The ingredients are breaded shrimp put up in a sauce. When you open the package, you find a few shrimp, heavily coated with greasy crumbs, boating about in sauce. If you complain that what you bought does not resemble the picture of what you thought you were buying, you have no case *if you had not followed the "Serving suggestion."* You are supposed to know that the shrimp could have looked "reasonably" like the picture if you had done what the manufacturer had done and suggested that you do — scrape all the greasy breadcrumbs off the shrimp, make a mound of the crumbs, and arrange the shrimp on the top of the mound. You have a case only if you can prove it is impossible to do what the manufacturer "suggested." Such sorts of weasel-worded trickery and quibbling indicate the daily difficulties of the federal enforcement agencies in their attempts to write regulations that would make honest men out of manufacturers.

Nevertheless, some progress has been made. Noncarbonated beverages that appear to contain either fruit or vegetable juice, but which in fact contain neither the one nor the other, must be clearly labeled as "containing no . . . juice," or "no . . . juice," or "does not contain . . . juice." The word "imitation" on a label will, under new regulations, henceforth mean the product is NOT as nutritious as the product it resembles and for which it is a sleazy substitute. (On the other hand, if you are a manufacturer and wish to slide around this so that you can put a fake butter on the market, all you need do is think up a brand name. Don't call it anything like "butter." You can have a picture on the box that looks rather like a stick of butter and reasonably like what is in the package, but be sure to call your product something like "Farmfresh Hi-Spred." You will have deceived no one — not, that is, in a strictly legal sense.)

Very well, there are loopholes. But the days of the unfinished comparative are passing from advertising. In the bad old days, Chiquita bananas were marketed under the slogan "keeps longer." It was quite true that a Chiquita banana might have "kept longer" than something else, such as a saucer of milk left out on a cow pasture under a hot sun on the Fourth of July, but not longer than any similar banana, and eventually the slogan had to be withdrawn. Under new regulations, food manufacturers will not be allowed to say "nourishing," "wholesome," or "packed with nourishment" unless the manufacturer specifically states just what is so nourishing and how nourishing it actually is, and any processed food laced with salts or sugar, in such amounts as to constitute a hazard to someone's health, will have to carry a disclosure of those amounts.

Frankly, I find all this depressing as hell. It may be true, as the FDA man said, that the housewife must become a label reader in order to survive, but to say this is also to demand that she know more than anyone can reasonably be expected to know, and to confess the government's inability to deal with a situation wherein anyone who goes to the supermarket runs a risk of being malnourished, possibly poisoned, and robbed. It is to speak volumes about the American condition.

We have evidently created a society so abstract that much of the very food we eat is an abstraction of food.

In this abstract society, we find all manner of middlemen standing between the farm gate and our dinner tables. Sometimes the government itself serves as a middleman to raise the price of the food we eat, as in the case of the sale of grain to the Soviet Union. Sometimes the middleman is a processor who increases the cost of food while decreasing its value. Some middlemen are speculators who do nothing at all to our food but raise its price; other middlemen are frankly criminals; some are cheats; and all of them are expensive if not also entirely unnecessary. In order to survive among these predators, the housewife is to defend herself by reading labels.

To Market, to Market, to Pay Through the Nose

Shopping with Kafka

Whooosh! go the electronic doors, and there is the sound of Muzak, and here are the aisles piled high with an apparent plenty of almost everything, and the actual best of almost nothing. The supermarket seems to be a leisurely temple of bountiful Ceres, but it is instead a sterile machine conceived by the kind of military mind that imagines beauty in terms of empty spaces, right angles, neatness, and obedience. Here are the commanding signs: "Frozen Foods — Section 36." Here is the totalitarian equality of the standard brand. Here is the disembodied voice of the loudspeaker that cannot be turned off. Here is efficiency — the maddening efficiency of the cans of identical soups that neatly flow from gravity-feed racks. It is impossible to enter a supermarket without being aware that you are in the thrall of an immense, anonymous corporate entity, infinitely cold and remote. You take what you are offered. If you ask for something you want but do not see, the store manager will put you in your place, for he is a *Gauleiter*. He and his underlings speak with the dispassionate accents of insect bureaucracy when they explain, "We don't carry it." With equal willingness, devotion, and efficiency, they could operate any other branch of the same, or any other, supermarket chain, be it in Denver, Berlin, Philadelphia, or Omsk.

And here we hunt in sullen lonely silence for our food; paying for the green stamps; paying for the misused food stamps; paying for the deceptive and misredeemed cents-off coupons; paying fees and kickbacks to crooks; paying for mountains of fingernail-proof plastic, tinfoil, glass, paper, cardboard, and tons of other trash — and paying for the bags to put the trash in; paying the price of being lied to, misled, and overcharged; paying all the costs of making money for anonymous corporations that systematically take whatever advantage they can of a naive and anonymous multitude; buying what we must because that is what there is and paying for it all the money that a devious sharpshooter in an alpaca jacket knows he can find in our pockets; paying for all this essentially because in the names of speed and convenience we have dispensed with human relationships. To shop in a supermarket is rather like shopping with Kafka.

Less than a lifetime ago, none of these excrescences existed. Just after the First World War, when there were still gas lamps on city streets, everyone who lived in a city bought his food at neighborhood shops, from carters, or at open-air markets. In those days, the shops put fresh sawdust thick on the floors each morning. Flour was kept in bins, as were rice and dried beans; pickles came in barrels, butter in wooden tubs, milk in glass bottles, and oysters in their shells. Game hung in the shops in season. Everyone knew the butcher and the grocer; the tradesmen knew their customers and their customers' desires; cards, if not presents, would be exchanged at Christmas time. Everyone shopped with a market basket, and, since little food was wrapped, there was little trash. Shopping was then very nearly as leisurely and humane as a stroll in the park during which you stop to chat with friends. Children loved to go shopping in those days, because the shopkeepers would give them fruit and candy.

There was no electrical refrigeration then, but most people, though by no means all of them, had iceboxes. If you had an icebox, you would put a card in the window for the iceman. The card told him how many pounds you wanted that day, and the iceman would chip five-, ten-, and twenty-pound cakes from the blocks of ice in his horse-drawn wagon. He would pick the cakes up with a pair of tongs and carry them over his leather-clad shoulder into the house and put them into the zinc-lined wooden icebox for you. If you did not have an icebox, it really did not matter so far as spoilage was concerned. You could keep the perishable foodstuffs in the cool cellar in summer or out on the back porch pantry in winter, and in any case they would not be there long, because you would shop for food at least four mornings in every week, if not every morning except Sunday. The pattern then was quite similar to the pattern still followed in European cities today: people shopped daily for fresh foods bought in the neighborhood from people they knew.

Today we shop differently because we live differently. The supermarket, like the food it sells, is a construct of the way we live. The supermarkets by no means owe their success wholly to their having driven small independent grocers out of business. Their success would have been impossible without the public's willingness to shop in supermarkets, and this in turn involved the public's choice in a manner of living that was made possible by popular acceptance of two inventions: the refrigerator and the automobile. While the whole matter may now seem as impossible to resolve as the question of which came first, the chicken or the egg, it can be said that the supermarket was not so much the child of Guile and Greed as it was born out of Opportunity by Circumstance.

If, for example, a household lacks refrigeration and a vehicle, its food supply must be local, or its shopping local and frequent, or both. No one wants to buy more food than will keep till used, and there is a limit as to how much bulk and weight anyone can hand-carry over any distance.

On the other hand, if a household has a means of storing a surplus of perishable foods, and if it has a vehicle capable of carrying a large amount of supplies rapidly over a considerable distance, then the household need not be within a convenient walking distance of its food supply, nor do the householders have to shop every day. In that case, they can live in one city neighborhood and drive all the way across town to shop in another where there is a supermarket that sells for less than the independent grocer charges close to home. They can load up the car with food for a week, and thereby save themselves both money and time. Indeed, given refrigeration and transportation, they need not live in the city at all. They can live in a suburban bedroom community five miles distant from the shopping center to which they drive once a week for their foodstuffs.

The refrigerator and the automobile are the critical factors in our equation. They are fundamentally responsible for our divorce from the land; for the ability of corporate farms in California to feed people in Maine. By opening the distance between the farm gate and the dinner table, they created an enormous room in which middlemen add their cost to our plates. The two inventions also made possible the existence of the modern metropolitan areas, with their suburban sprawls and shopping centers, and so had much to do with reshaping our pattern of living and determining our diets. Moreover, the automobile and the refrigerator are indirectly responsible for the decay of center city businesses in that the creation of the suburban shopping center worked to the economic disadvantage of center city stores.

The suburbia that appeared after the Second World War was and is absolutely predicated upon the automobile. And because of the automobile, there was no need to insert corner groceries into every so many suburban blocks. One great center, surrounded by a parking lot the approximate size of Delaware, could serve thousands of arriving automobilists motoring in from any of several suburban housing developments. It could also serve automobilists arriving from the center city, and when they thought about this and considered the differences in rents and taxes between city and county and the plentitude of suburban parking space as against the paucity of city parking space, the proprietors of many city businesses, including those in the food business, saw nothing but gold in the concept of the suburban shopping center. Great department stores moved to the suburbs, pursuing those customers who had once lived in the city and confident that other of their customers who still lived there would, perforce, drive out to the suburban store. The national supermarket chains found natural homes in the suburban shopping centers that ministered to captive markets several miles wide. Meanwhile, having killed off the small independent competition, they reduced the number of their city stores while enlarging the size of those that remained there.

The emergent economic law of our technological society is this: The larger the population, the smaller the number of stores. Today, most Americans buy most, if not virtually all, of their food from supermarkets for the very good reason that most people have nowhere else to shop and/or because the surviving independent specialty grocers must charge more for their foods than most people can pay. The supermarkets keep the variety of their offerings to a minimum, and, in each market area, charge all that the traffic in that area will bear. A supermarket in one city neighborhood will charge $1.89 for a pound of bacon. Another supermarket, a branch store of the same chain, doing business in the same city but in another neighborhood, will charge $2.05 for a pound of that same brand of bacon if it can get away with it. The supermarkets are not insensitive to the public's demand for products or to the public's reaction to prices, but they are not responsive to individuals. They sell massfood to massman, and it is for precisely this reason that the massive supermarket is able to get away with several varieties of mass murder.

So much for the argument; let us proceed to the evidence. But while we examine the evidence of cheap trickery and opulent tawdriness, I suggest we keep in mind the fact that the supermarkets are not unique. They are another manifestation of giantism — of the kind of giantism that helps form the massman by reducing the possibility of one man's meeting another face to face in the ordinary commerce of life. Just as we have giant school systems remote from public control, just as we have unions remote from the members' participation, just as we have businesses remote from even the nominal control of stockholders, and governments over which most people believe they have no control, so do we have these giant stores, which reflect, as much as they help to mold, the way we live.

I think we did not choose to live the way we do so much as we slipped into it, ever so innocently and pleasurably following personal convenience, novelty, and the pleasant prospect of saving both time and money through invention, being always delighted to discover immediate advantage. In the process, we quite unknowingly began to dig graves for more people than the corner grocer with whom we once exchanged Christmas cards and the iceman with his horse and wagon. When we unwittingly let slip a system of personal relationships and a pattern of neighboring, we unknowingly and relentlessly moved deeper into a strange, impersonal world that did not seem to be a world we made. The supermarket is a construct of that world, and so is its food, and we certainly could get along very well without either of them if we chose to live differently. It is just a thought to take along; but now allow me to step on the treadle and whooosh open that magic door . . .

That's What's So Special About Them

It is the glory and triumph of the American supermarket to have made more food, of more kinds, available to more people at lower cost than any marketing system heretofore seen on the face of the earth. Such at least is the opinion of our supermarket executives, who add that their margins of profit are so paper-thin as to be virtually nonexistent. Their margin is less than a penny on the dollar, they say, and, even though food prices are high, they are nonetheless giving us food practically at cost.

Another view of the supermarkets is that of the Federal Trade Commission. What FTC says suggests to me that, in addition to the enormous profits they make, the supermarkets steal no less than $2600 million from us every year — through overcharges alone. By this, the FTC refers to false weights and measures and other deceitful business practices, and not to whatever mistakes cash register operators may make by hitting the wrong keys.

My view of our supermarkets is that I don't care half so

much about what they earn or steal as I care about the moral swamp in which they operate. I am insulted and outraged when these people take us for fools, presuming that we know nothing about food, that we shop impulsively and irrationally, that we can be cheated with impunity and misled into wasting our money on trash. That is their attitude; that is their view of you and me; and if you step over here to the meat counter, I will show you what I mean:

Chuck Roast, 87¢; California Roast, blade in, $1.03; Cross Rib Pot Roast, $1.39; Under Blade Pot Roast, 99¢; Arm Pot Roast, bone in, $1.29; Chuck Roast, boneless, $1.27; Arm Steak, $1.18; London Broil, $1.53; Cube Steak, $1.49; Stewing Cubes, $1.59; Chuck Steak, 87¢.

You will notice that all of these meats are marked SPECIALS! Now, this store advertises its employment of "Master Butchers."

"The quality of every cut of meat is backed by the signature of a Master Butcher," the advertising says. "Behind every great cut of meat there's one of our 108 Master Butchers. He puts his signature on each cut he's responsible for. Proudly. Because he knows there isn't a meat case in town that holds better value than his. In quality. In trim. He has seen to that — personally. Get to know the name of your Master Butcher. Better yet, get to know him."

Better still, try to find him. If you do, you will learn that his mastery lies in creative writing as much as it does in butchery. All of the meats we see in this case — the SPECIALS! of the Master Butcher — all of these apparently different cuts at their different prices happen to be chuck cut in slightly different ways. The fact that chuck steak is offered at the same price as chuck roast may possibly have been due to oversight. No one is perfect. In any case, all of it is eighty-seven-cents chuck. By masterful butchery and inventive naming, every five dollars' worth of chuck has become twelve dollars' worth of it.

And here is another meat counter, full of packages of grayish-pink hamburger. You see a sign over this display, saying that the hamburger has been "extended" by the addition of textured vegetable protein. This means that protein taken from soybeans has been added to the meat. But the sign fails to say what percentage of the hamburger is soybean. And you will notice that the individually wrapped packages fail to say there is any at all. Instead, their labels say, "MEAT: Beef, 50%; Pork, 25%; Poultry, 25%."

Here is a third meat counter, where the Master Butcher is offering us top round steak at $1.69 and a steak called "Bracciole" at $1.83. Bracciole is a top round steak cut thin. Look at the "Quick Fry Pork Chops!" They cost twenty cents more per pound than the other pork chops, the difference being that, as in the case of the Bracciole, they have been cut thin. Oh, now here they have porterhouse steak at $2.29, tenderloin at $3.99, and sirloin strip at $2.99. The tenderloin and the sirloin come from the same porterhouse. So we can buy the porterhouse at $2.29 — and remove the bone at home if we want the tenderloin one night and the sirloin another, or we could pay the Master Butcher $2.40 to cut out the T-bone for us. Come to think of it, that service costs more than the price per pound of the steak. And, since it would take the Master Butcher just as long to remove the T-bone from a three-pound porterhouse as it would for him to remove the T-bone from a two-pound one, namely, about ten seconds, the rate the store is charging for this boning service is higher than the hourly rate a Park Avenue psychiatrist would charge a patient. Look! There is another SPECIAL. This one says "SPECIAL! No Tenderloin Removed!" How true that is. No tenderloin has been removed for the very good reason there is no tenderloin to be removed from that cut.

What the store thinks of us is now very clear. It believes that we cannot tell the difference between a chuck steak and an off hind hoof and that we cannot reason. It also believes we cannot do arithmetic. For example, you may have seen those bags of onions piled up near the turnstiles as we entered the store. The three-pound bags marked "79¢"? Today's SPECIAL! on onions? Well, now over here, in the produce counters, there is a bin of loose onions. They are identical to the ones in the bags. But they are priced at twenty-five cents a pound. The people who run this store must have nothing but contempt for us.

Down the street there is another supermarket. This chain advertises that it is honest. "We Don't Play Games!" its advertisement says. We can therefore reasonably deduce that all supermarkets are precisely as honorable as all used-car salesmen. In this store we find a special sale of mushrooms at forty-nine cents, but when we take the mushrooms to the checkout counter, the girl rings up ninety-eight cents. When we protest, she shows us her chart of prices posted beside her machine. Sure enough, on her chart mushrooms are ninety-eight cents. But the sign on the produce bin said "49¢." When we point this fact out to her, she gives us the mushrooms for forty-nine cents, saying that "they never tell us about specials." If someone is not playing games, then someone is making mistakes that happen to be profitable ones.

Call it Penn Fruit, call it Pantry Pride, call it Giant Plastic, or call it what you will. So far as I am concerned, if you have seen one supermarket, you have seen them all, and one by any name can make as many mistakes as any other. Just before Thanksgiving, my wife and I went to a Safeway that advertised a special sale of turkeys. We went on Tuesday, and there were the birds, on sale at the advertised price, piled in the common grave of a frozen-food locker. We had not thought of buying a *frozen* turkey, but that was the only turkey being sold, and the price was attractively low. As a

matter of prudent self-defense, we read the label on a
plastic-wrapped bird. The label stated the price per pound,
the weight of the turkey, and the price of the turkey. The
multiplication was correct. We bought the bird, intending to
thaw it that night and Wednesday, to begin the cooking
Wednesday night, and finish the cooking on Thanksgiving
Day.

On Wednesday afternoon we unwrapped the now-thawed
bird and found another plastic wrapper beneath the outer
one. This, too, had a label, put on by the processor, stating
the weight of the turkey. This weight was three pounds less
than the weight stated on the wrapper Safeway had superim-
posed upon the processor's wrapper. Put on the bathroom
scales, the turkey proved to weigh exactly what the processor
said it did. We had bought three pounds' worth of nonexistent turkey. We could hardly take it back; the store was now
closed till Friday. Our holiday was somewhat less thankful
than it might have been.

When we took the two wrappers back to the supermarket
on Friday, the store's reaction was interesting. First, it
seemed the manager was unavailable. It was not until the
following Wednesday that we found him and cornered him
behind a display of canned fruit juice.

"Oh, that's the meat department," he explained. "We
don't have anything to do with them; they're a separate
concession."

Where was the head of the meat department? Well, he was
on vacation and no one knew when he would be back or
even where he went. Anyway, it was probably all a mistake,
the store manager said. Sorry, no refund. You have to see
the meat department manager about that.

It might seem as if we had cause for suit, but upon what
grounds? Malice? Oversight? The two plastic wrappers
meant nothing without the turkey, and even had we brought

the turkey and the bags into court, how could we prove that the bird we brought to court was the bird that had been in either of the two plastic bags? And who would bring suit over such a small sum, anyway?

We returned to that Safeway, moved now by curiosity, not hunger. This time we discovered that the meat department, perhaps because of the manager's continued absence on vacation, had fallen from its high standard of arithmetical excellence. The stated weights of every piece of meat we tested on their scales were precisely what the labels said they were, but when the weights were multiplied by the stated price per pound, it appeared that the store had made grievous errors in every case, and all of them happened to be in the store's favor.

The butcher's thumb has been on the scale at least as long as there have been butchers, but it now would seem the weight of the thumb can be programmed into the computer that prints out the price labels. By mistake, of course.

Sometimes mistakes are made in meaning. There is a seafood supply house that advises its client stores that turbot looks like a cross between a halibut and a fluke, and that turbot fillets could therefore "be used as you would fluke or sole." One store's interpretation of this advice was to sell *halibut* fillets as "lemon sole" and "Dover sole" — at sole prices. Likewise, rounds punched from skate wings became "scallops" and crayfish became "baby lobster tails."

There is also a store that cuts wheels of cheddar into wedges, and mistakenly wraps the wedges in differently tinted plastic, selling them at different prices under the names "sharp," "old sharp," and "aged sharp." The large crumbs caused by the cutting are mistakenly put into small plastic bags and sold at an even higher price as "cheese bits."

Who the devil thinks these mistakes are clever? Or that

they are good for business? Or, in the larger sense, that they are good for America? Presumably the people who think such ploys are clever are the very same people who add a psychological surcharge to the $2600 million that the FTC says they steal from us every year through their false weights, substitutions, misrepresentations, and garden-variety low trickery. Presumably they are the supermarket managers, whose contemptuous view of us as a mass of ovine, captive easy marks includes the notion that we are also impulsive and irrational ones. Having made what can only be called a scholarly study of consumer buying habits, the supermarket managers have designed both the store floor plans and the displays to serve as psychological traps.

For example, knowing children to be what they are, which is bored, restless, and wishing they were somewhere else than in the store, the clever store manager will have put candy and other juvenile junk food on bottom shelves in easy view of little eyes and within the reach of tiny hands. The children will reach for it and, the manager believes, the parents will let them keep the junk they snatch for fear of starting a row by telling the children to put it back.

The store will be laid out so as to bring the shoppers first to the high-profit items, because a study has proved that shoppers begin filling their carts when they come to the first displays of the foods they seek. Thus large displays of the higher-profit foods will be located at adult arm-and-eye level at the ends of the aisles. The lower-profit ones will be found in smaller displays in the middle of the aisles and/or on shelves above and below normal arm-and-eye levels.

Knowing the shoppers' penchant for impulse buying, the manager arranges for the impulse items, such as soft drinks, snacks, and what are called "gourmet foods," to be placed across the ends of the aisles and close to the checkout chutes.

Another kind of impulse purchase is that of the "go-togethers." If a store puts on a loss-leader sale of broccoli, and if the manager has his wits filed sharp, then next to the loss-leader broccoli there will be extremely high-profit bottles of hollandaise sauce.

Presuming the public is unobservant or unthinking or both, a store will put on special display something that is regularly sold — such as advertising "SPECIAL! Three cans for 60¢!" when each can is marked at twenty cents.

By a somewhat similar deceit, a supermarket may advertise a sale on one brand of salad oil. And in the store there will be a large placard also announcing this sale. But beneath the placard there will be a huge display of some other brand of much more expensive salad oil. The brand to which the advertisement and the placard refer may be found on a shelf display two-bottles wide in a farther aisle among the Harvard beets.

What these practices have in common with out-and-out cheating is that both are predicated upon a perversion of psychology. It may very well be true, as studies of consumer shopping habits suggest, that the general public is ignorant, unobservant, easily misled, impulsive, and irrational. But it is one thing to make scientific note of this, and quite a different thing to use this knowledge deliberately to take vicious commercial advantage; to create a store that is a trap; to create situations scientifically designed to lead people to act irrationally; to sneak to wring the most money out of the least thoughtful and the least informed — who, by the way, are also likely to be the least able to pay the price. One wonders who these store managers can be, what they can possibly think of what they are doing, and what they can think of themselves.

A man I shall discreetly call Oswald Krell was most helpful in answering these very questions. Together with his wife, Krell owns and operates a somewhat less than super market that is in competition with three gigantic ones. He has been in the marketplace ever since starting as a stock boy thirty-five years ago. Krell laughed when I told him about the SPECIAL! on the three-pound bags of onions that each cost four cents more than three pounds of loose onions.

"Ah, that's merchandising," he said, and chuckled. "It's that four cents, that's what's so special about them.

"Look," he said seriously, "you show me where in the law it says that if you mark something 'special' it has to mean it's specially *low*. Maybe it means it's specially *high*. 'Special' doesn't have to mean any price, high or low. All it means is, it's special; there's something special about it. All the store was saying is that those onions were special, and that's what they were: special."

By the same logic, it now appeared that sixty cents for three twenty-cent cans *was* special, because if you multiply three times twenty, you come out at sixty and never at any other figure. So sixty cents was the unique and special price.

And so with respect to the soybean-hamburger patties. The labels on the patties were correct in their reference to the *meat* the patties contained. If the customer read the sign over the case, he would know that the patties also contained soybeans.

Krell saw nothing wrong with the idea of selling the same part of a steer at several different prices under several different names. "Ah, that's merchandising," he said again. It was not really overcharging, because it was a service to the customer.

"You take a bone out for a customer and you do him a service, so you charge for the service."

Krell readily agreed that any customer who wanted to cut up his own chickens and roasts at home could save nearly $1000 a year by doing so, but instead of seeing the store's fees as unreasonable, if not grotesque, he said that just went to show how valuable the store's services were.

Because I was one of his customers and because I evinced

a serious interest in marketing and was eager to learn, Krell was glad to tell me what he knew. A series of conversations ensued over a period of weeks, and at the first of these, I wondered how he and his wife could operate a small, independent supermarket in direct competition with three gigantic chain stores in the same section of the city, particularly when his fixed costs were relatively higher than theirs, and when he had to charge more for many items than the huge stores charged for those same items. Part of the answer, he said, lay in personal service.

Unlike the giant stores, Oswald Krell's store will take telephoned orders and make deliveries. He will cash checks for regular customers. At Christmas time he sets out liquor and cheeses, cookies and meats for his customers. He allows charge accounts. He keeps an excellent line of meats, and his butchers will cut, trim, and bone to order. There is seldom a long line at either of his two checkout counters. Krell makes a point of remembering names, and as a result of the courtesies and services it finds in his store, his clientele is willing to pay his often higher-than-giant-supermarket prices. The rest of the answer, however, lay in the other supermarket prices, which seemed quite adequately high to permit anyone to stay in business.

Each morning Krell receives from his supplier a printed statement showing what every store in the city has paid for its supplies that day, together with the prices they are charging their customers. He showed me such a statement. Generally speaking, the figures were sufficiently identical to suggest telepathy, if not collusion. Different prices on some of the same brands and items did obtain in different sections of the city, however, and often enough within the same chain of stores. When asked about this, Krell explained that every store charges all it can get.

"Like take produce," Krell said. "Now here, you see my markup on produce averages thirty-four percent. I know, that's low, but you know the kind of stuff they send me — it's terrible — and anyway, that's not where the money is. But take produce. Now, if I had the store in Crestwood Hills, I could mark it up a hundred percent, because those people up there have so much money they don't care and anyway, they'd never know the difference. Your markup depends on the neighborhood."

Krell showed me his books. His markup on meat was 25 percent; on canned goods and staples, 14 percent; frozen foods, 25 percent. The overall average markup on all items in the store was only 18 percent. This figure seemed in line with what could be deduced from the daily reports of supermarket wholesale prices and retail markups. As Krell explained, he could not afford to get too far out of line. He turned next to a daily report from New York City, which, he said, comes out "like on a stock ticker." The report tells the daily changes in wholesale prices.

"Now you know you're not supposed to change the price once you put the item on the shelf," he said. "So what you do is put two cans of it on the shelf, and you keep the other five hundred cases of it in the basement. So you look at the ticker, and it says fruit cocktail is fifty-one cents a can today, up three cents from yesterday, and you remember that you paid forty cents last week for all those cans in the basement. So as soon as you sell the two cans off the shelf, or throw them away, you go down in the basement. Today's wholesale price is fifty-one cents, so you add your fourteen-percent markup for canned goods, and you put the can on the shelf for fifty-eight cents, and now you're selling a forty-cent can for fifty-eight cents. There's no law that says you can't buy when it's cheap and not display it till the price goes up. People do it all the time. It's what business is all about; you make a little money.

"You know," he said, "the prices on the ticker change from day to day, and sometimes in the same day. People have actually won and lost fortunes in prune juice. Don't ask me why, I don't know, but for a while the price of prune juice was going up and down like a yo-yo, and people were betting in prune juice."

He opened a book of audited accounts. They showed what he had paid for electricity, rent, heat, legal fees, accounting fees, wages, truck deliveries, telephone calls, supplies; all the costs of doing business were there displayed.

"This is for nineteen sixty-two," Krell explained, "because if I showed you the books for last year, you'd never come back to the store."

We laughed about that.

The audited account showed that Oswald Krell realized in 1962 a net profit, after deducting costs and taxes, of slightly more than $25,000. That was what he and his wife cleared. This did not seem a princely recompense for their six-day weeks of twelve-hour days. It did, however, indicate that if he and his wife could eke this out on a relatively small business with a relatively high overhead, then it was quite possible for the owners and operators of huge supermarkets, which had relatively small overheads, to live a bit more comfortably than Mr. and Mrs. Oswald Krell.

"Of course there's money in it," Krell agreed. "I've been in this business thirty-five years. You asked me who's primarily responsible for the high price of food today, and out of my experience, I'll tell you this: it's the stores. And particularly it's the big food processors who also own the chain stores, and smart guys like that one who set up Tremendous Kitchens as an outfit in the middle between the processor and the Giant Plastic stores that Tremendous Kitchens owns."

I asked him to explain.

"Well, OK," he said. "So your wife buys Junkies, those corn things? The wholesale price of Junkies is twenty cents. So this guy orders Junkies by the ton, for Tremendous

Kitchens. So the Junkie people give him five percent off — if you're a big guy, you call it a discount and you're a businessman; if you're a little guy, they call it a kickback and you're a crook, right? Anyway, he sells those Junkies to his Giant Plastic stores at the wholesale price, twenty cents a bag, so he's made five percent, selling to himself. But then Giant Plastic marks up the bags, thirty-six cents apiece, they make sixteen cents a bag. The Giant Plastic stores got to make money or they wouldn't be in business. But Giant Plastic is making money for Tremendous Kitchens as well as making money for Giant Plastic, right? And this guy owns *both?* Plus he's getting his five percent when he buys from Junkies and sells to Plastic? If you think he's going to give that five percent to the customer, you're out of your mind. What the hell, it's a business."

We discussed, briefly, an article that had appeared in the morning newspaper. The president of a supermarket chain had told a meeting of stockholders that food retailers were being subjected to "unwarranted and unjustified" criticism on profits. He was quoted as saying that retail food profits "are too low to provide a proper return on the capital investment necessary to operate in today's competitive climate" and that "if we eliminated all the retail food profits," the customer would benefit only to the extent of eight cents per person per week.

Krell burst into a roar of laughter.

"That's the guy!" he said, and laughed again. "That's the guy I was telling you! He's the one who owns Tremendous Kitchens and Giant Plastic! Listen, I know the guy; he's a member of our country club. Look what else the article says. Tremendous Kitchens' earnings were eight point nine million last year, which is up two point seven million over the year before — and while he's telling the stockholders this, he's talking about eight cents a week per customer is all that Giant Plastic is making. But Plastic is making money for

Tremendous, as well as for Plastic. Eight cents a week; he's got to be kidding."

When one has the wit and wisdom of an Oswald Krell as a guide, the wonderful world of the supermarket begins to take on a new meaning, and the accounts appearing in the press become more intelligible. Thus, when the *New York Times* reported that the Grocery Manufacturers of America estimated that their member concerns were being cheated out of $200 million a year through "misredemption" of their newspaper and magazine cents-off coupons, Krell warned me not to be naive — and therefore not to believe that it is either the food processors or the stores who are actually losing all that money. The costs of doing business are always passed on to the customer. Even if the coupons were not misredeemed, he said, they would still add to the price of the products, because they are a form of advertising. The more heavily anything is advertised, the more expensive it becomes. So the customer does not really receive "cents off" when presenting the grocer with a coupon, even if this seems to be the case. The customer is really paying the cost of being told he is buying a bargain. As for misredemption itself, Krell had a story to tell.

"OK, now a guy came in the other day, and said 'Are you the owner?' and I said, 'I'm the manager.' Because you don't want to tell a guy everything you know, right? Anyway, I'm the manager, too, so I said I was the manager.

"He had a whole suitcase full of coupons. Now, OK, coupons, like food stamps, are a pain in the ass to me, right? But they're like money. I send the coupons to the manufacturer, and the manufacturer sends me back the money. This guy wants to sell me the whole suitcase for fifty percent. Now, I'm no saint, you know what I mean?

"Anyway, you can imagine what would happen if I sent Parkay coupons for two thousand pounds of their margarine when I don't even carry it in the store? So I told the guy to get lost, but we talked a little bit first. You know what? He'd quit his job, because now he was making two to three hundred a week selling coupons at half-price to store managers. He spends all week cutting coupons out of newspapers and magazines and then he goes to supermarket managers and makes a deal. He makes fifty, they make fifty, and who's to know? If you're a manager in one of those big stores, like Giant Plastic, you can get rid of those coupons all right. You send them to a clearing-house that weighs them and sends you the money.

"Now your wife buys *Woman's Day*, right? She pays thirty-five cents for it. But that magazine is worth a dollar-eighty in coupons. When she buys that magazine, she's actually making a dollar-forty-five. That's why she can't go to a Giant Plastic and buy a copy of *Woman's Day* because there aren't any left. You think women bought them? Don't be naive. The manager bought them. He clips out all the coupons. The big supermarkets can't keep them on the rack because the managers buy them or the checkout people steal them.

"It's like food stamps," Krell said, shaking his head in rueful recognition of the way things are. "You think food stamps are for poor people? Yeah, poor people in Cadillacs come to the store. You can walk up and down the avenue and buy all the food stamps you want. The poor guy puts up sixty dollars for his stamps, right? Then the bank gives him a hundred dollars' worth of stamps. So he's forty bucks ahead, right? So what's he do with it, buy food? Don't be silly. He sells the stamps, and spends the forty on booze; he buys lottery tickets; he goes to the races. Or maybe he comes to my store and says, 'Look, I'll let you have them for eighty.' So he doesn't make forty; he makes twenty and you make twenty, right?

"Now you know I'm not a saint, but why take a chance on twenty bucks when there's a five-hundred-dollar fine if they catch you? But I'm a small guy. Take a big guy, the manager of one of those really big stores; so if he was caught he'd never miss the five hundred dollars, he's making so much on the side on those stamps, you know? Besides from being a pain in the ass for me to have to take in stamps from people who do buy food with them, and keep an account, those stamps are like money and the whole thing is a rip-off and you and I and everybody who pays taxes are paying for it."

As Krell told his stories, it appeared there might be even more reasons for the price of supermarket food being what it was than could be attributed to crookedness, deceit, collusion, and misredemption. He had mentioned his membership in a country club. His home was near the club. He was a man in his middle fifties who wore his hair youthfully long, and dressed in closefitting doubleknit slacks, colorful sport jackets, and Florentine shoes with square gold buckles on them. His wife, too, was fashionably turned out. Every year they took a winter vacation at Acapulco and a summer holiday in Europe. On every working day they would arrive at their store at seven in the morning in their long, white Cadillac, put on blue smocks provided for the store by a laundry service, put their smocks in the laundry hamper at seven in the evening, turn out the lights, lock the store, and go home in their Cadillac, which was always new each year and always white. They worked long and hard for their money, but they seemed to live rather well on what they earned.

Then one day matters came into sharper focus when a salesman entered the store. He represented a bakery specializing in French bread, and after a few minutes he left without having made a sale.

"You know, those people are very naive," Krell mused as we watched the salesman depart. "They have a good product; I'm not knocking the product; but you know they didn't give me one loaf of bread, not even one roll? How do they expect to do business like that? Now when the Humble Pie Farms guy comes in, he says 'I want you to have these five hundred loaves you can give away to your customers so they'll try them.' You know what I mean?"

"Yes. It means he gives you five hundred free loaves that you can sell for fifty-five cents apiece."

"That's right," Krell said. "I mean you're not naive, Humble Pie isn't naive, I'm not naive. But those French bread people, how naive can you get?"

He paused to wonder about this.

"I'll be honest with you," he said. "You know how much I make on milk? I make enough on milk alone to pay the mortgage on the house and buy a new car every year. You know how it works? You say to the dairy, OK, I'll sell only your products, right? Then you sell so many quarts over a certain number, and a guy comes around and hands you five percent in cash. If they don't show that cash on their books, which they don't, you don't have to show it on yours, right? What it is, you call it a kickback. The customer comes in and he thinks milk costs so much a bottle; all over town that's the price of milk. *He* thinks. The customer doesn't know what milk costs. The farmer might not be getting any money, but the dairies are making money so fast they give you five percent. I was very naive about milk till I was talking with some guys and they say, 'Ossie, are you stupid or something, you don't ask for five percent?' That's how I learned. You have to ask for it. So I asked, and the guy comes around with the five percent in cash.

"It's like with cigarettes," Krell said. "For every carton you order, they give you two free packs. At fifty cents a pack, they give you a dollar, right? So you order twenty cartons, and what the customer doesn't know, and naturally what the IRS doesn't know, is you get twenty-four cartons, a gift of twenty dollars. I ask you, are the cigarette people making money? Are the dairies and the bread people making money? They're making so much money they can give it away."

If milk paid the mortgage and bought the car, then it was likely that cigarettes paid for Acapulco and bread paid for Europe, or maybe it was just that all those cans in the basement paid for everything and that Oswald Krell was actually more of a saint than he wished to appear at the country club. In any case, someone was ultimately paying for the gifts that Krell received, and it was not particularly difficult to imagine who was ultimately picking up the bill. Nor was it difficult to imagine what gifts might be given to entrepreneurs much more powerful than such a small operator as Oswald Krell.

It next appeared there was another charge hidden in the price of food these days, and Krell was growing sick with worry about it.

"You want to know why food is so high, part of it is because of the kind of people there are these days," he said. "Take Giant Plastic down the street. You know what they lose each year? Fifty thousand dollars in rip-offs. It doesn't sound like big money in a store like that, but it's still fifty thousand so they add what they lose to the price of the food. How else? Now you see they have these uniformed guards that look like state cops with guns in the store. The same as Market Plenty has: guards with guns. You buy a dozen oranges, and you also pay people to stand around with guns. You want to be in business today, you got to have a gun.

"There are a lot of times when I want to get out of the business," Krell said. "It's a lot of work, a lot of headaches. Every time there's a new food on television one night, I have to have it in the store next morning; the people expect it. Then about six-thirty when we're closing down, people come in and rip you off. You know, I never thought I'd see the day, but I'm going to carry a gun. So the next guy like that — and you can tell by the way they look — the next guy who comes into the store just when we're closing, I'll just pull my jacket aside and let him see the gun."

I made some inane remark about the price of guns and butter, and Krell took it seriously.

"You're right," he said. "You know, if you want to keep the cost of food down, the cheapest thing you can do is shred up some nice crisp dollar bills and put a little oil and vinegar, salt and pepper on them."

While the conversations with Krell touched upon a man's life and work, it seemed to me they essentially revealed a man making what way he could while contending with circumstances over which he had no control and that were certainly none of his devising. He was different from other supermarket store managers in that he and his wife owned their business, and therefore had a more direct interest in it than the salaried managers of corporate chains. This they expressed in the personal services they offered their customers, the services that were largely responsible for their ability to remain in business in competition with huge stores that sold many foodstuffs at prices lower than their own. But otherwise, Krell, like the larger supermarketeers, accepted the terms of a system that told him he was a businessman dealing with the public — as different from accepting a system of values that would have told him he was a grocer dealing with neighbors. Granted that the neighborhood grocer is a businessman, too. Yet there is a difference between a big business dealing with an anonymous public mass and a small business dealing with recognizable individuals.

Krell had accepted the outlook of big business in that he

shared the view that he was free to do anything the law did not expressly prohibit. If the law was silent with respect to the meaning of the word *special,* then he was free to give the word his own meaning. His store, too, was laid out as a psychological trap for the customers to whom he otherwise provided courtesies and services — and he thought this was clever. He almost, but not quite, equated sharp practice with dishonesty. His view was rather like that of a great university that hires ringers for its football team and pretends that they are scholars; it is a view that lacks a moral base. It embraces the notions *If the other guys can get away with it, so can I* and *You're stupid if you don't do it.* Whatever is advantageous is seen as intelligent, and whatever is disadvantageous is seen as stupid, and advantage is measured in terms of dollars and cents.

At bottom, if a moral swamp can be said to have a bottom, is the notion that business is a game and that the point of playing a game is to win it. Since this is a prevalent American point of view, it is scarcely surprising that Krell should share it. Questions might be asked as to whether the game should be played at all, since there is no question as to who the losers are.

One of the losers was seen using a pocket calculator to keep track of her purchases and to have a record that could be compared with the charges at the checkout counter, because, she explained, "You have to watch the store.

"You know," she said, "this is not my idea of a real good way to spend all Saturday morning. Stop that, Johnny, Mommy's talking! We'll be going in a minute! But last year we were spending thirty dollars a week for food. This year we're spending fifty, and everything is going up except my husband's salary because he has like a contract. I mean, something's got to give, and it can't be the rent, it can't be the taxes, it can't be the payments on the car, it can't be gasoline because my husband has to use the car to get to work and gas is going up. We turn the thermostat down and we don't waste electricity, but those bills keep going up anyway. So the food has to come down, and the only way to keep it down is, you know, Watch out! And try to find something cheaper."

A Defensive Alternative

It is widely believed that the supermarkets are able to sell food more cheaply than anyone else because they can buy huge shipments of foodstuffs at discount prices and make money on the thinnest of profit margins by doing a tremendous volume of business. Like many things that are widely believed, this is not precisely true. It is more accurate to say maybe they could if they did but they don't. A spokesman for the Pantry Pride supermarket chain explained the actual pricing policy thus:

"People have to have food, and they will pay the price. I'll be frank to say that people are buying close to their vests this year. We have reduced tonnage sales this year. Meats are down, definitely, while pasta and fish are up, but overall the tonnage is down, and our sales curve is down since last year. We earned less than a fifteen percent increase in profits last year. No doubt about it, people are buying less food. But this hasn't affected prices. Prices are up because people still have money."

He saw nothing wrong with raising the price of food as demand fell. That, he said, is what the automobile companies do; if you are dealing with something everyone needs, then the less they buy of it, the more it will cost them. So, at any rate, it seemed to me he was saying as he developed his views on contemporary economics. His views suggested that, in addition to whatever sorts of games supermarkets might be playing, the prices they charged might be uniformly and artificially high; that they were overcharging in the sense that they were pegging their prices not at profitable levels, but at extortionate ones.

It was a point that might be nailed down by comparison shopping, provided that some other market could be found that also offered a general selection of meats, seafood, dairy products, and vegetable produce to the general urban public. There are farmers' markets in many cites, but they are not always general markets; they are apt to be expensive ones selling specialty foodstuffs. But general farmers' markets are found in some cities, and one in Philadelphia was chosen for purposes of comparison for two reasons. First, according to federal statistics Philadelphia's cost of living is lower than that of any other major city. Second, Philadelphia is still partially served by a hinterland that produces a general selection of foodstuffs. If it should appear that the prices charged in the Philadelphia market were substantially lower than the prices charged in that city's cheapest chain supermarket, this would then call into question the vaunted efficiency, if not the honesty, of supermarket operations.

A comparison could be made on items that, chosen at random, would include meat, fish, fruits, and vegetables. Then, since convenience and the pocketbook are always factors in shopping, the comparison would be made between a branch of the cheapest supermarket, located in a lower-middle-class neighborhood, to which the shoppers could walk, and the farmers' market to which those same shoppers could not walk, but to which they would have to drive.

The Philadelphia farmers' market proved to be an open-air one that runs for five blocks along both sides of a narrow, one-way street in the heart of Philadelphia's Little Italy. The street is always squalid with litter; the sidewalks are always jammed with slowly moving shoppers and noisy with the cries of hucksters calling the prices of their wares. The street is otherwise filled with the colors and scents of Italy: the many colors of piles of fruits and vegetables, the scents of freshly ground espresso coffee and of Italian cheeses. Behind the open stalls that line the curbs there are small shops containing open barrels of pickled artichoke hearts, olives black and green, red and yellow peppers. Strings of onions, garlic, and chickpeas hang from ceilings together with all manner of cheeses. Here you can find patna rice, chestnuts and chestnut flour, many kinds of salad greens including fennel. One shop sells nothing but spices. There are rabbits, goats, and lambs hanging in their fur from butchers' hooks, and in the meat shops you find genuine prosciutto, stuffed pigs' feet, and all the European offerings of sausages, heads, tripe, brains, sweetbreads, hearts, kidneys, and livers. There is a cackle of live poultry in crates: ducks, chickens, geese, turkeys, and guinea hens. The mussels, clams, oysters, and crabs are all alive-o; the eyes and gills of the fin fish indicate they have come that day from the nearby New Jersey waters or those of Chesapeake Bay. There are shops selling homemade pasta fresh that morning, and two bakeries selling fresh-baked breads and pastries. In among the food shops are merchants who sell from clotheslines the kind of slacks and dresses that cost $1.29. It is for all the world a genuine Italian open-air market, a larger one than you will see in many an Italian city, but one with American local color: shops bear signs reading, "This store is Mafia staff car protected — You keepa you hands off" and "E meglio vivere un giorno come uno leone da cento anni come un' agnello: Mussolini."

The market's clientele, eddying through the choked street, consists of local residents, college students, artsy-craftsy hippies, blacks, and tweed-and-fur-bearing people who come from Philadelphia's elegant Main Line to find the ingredients for their European cuisine. The local residents patronize the market because it is located in their neighborhood and because it carries foods familiar to them. The wealthy come because the food is good. The students, bohemians, and blacks shop there because the food is not only good, but inexpensive. Many of the specialties, imported from Italy, are anything but inexpensive, but these are in every way exceptions to the rule.

I wandered up and down each side of this five-block-long street, bemused by the tremendous variety of foodstuffs, but confining my notations to the prices of only those foods that could also be purchased at the supermarket in the lower-middle-class neighborhood that was eight miles away. Apart from this restriction, the selection was purely at random. I noted the prices of mushrooms, lettuce, bacon, eggs, apples, lemons, melons, green beans, potatoes, tomatoes, peaches, bananas, asparagus, broccoli, celery, onions, parsley, artichokes, ham, spinach, shrimp, and nectarines.

A pound of bacon in the Italin market cost $1.49, which was ten cents less than the supermarket charged for a pound of the same brand of bacon. Lemons that the supermarket sold for fifteen cents apiece were sold for two cents apiece in the Italian market. Tomatoes that cost forty-nine cents a pound in the supermarket cost twenty-five cents in the Italian one, and the open-air market's tomatoes were fresh, ripe, and locally grown, whereas those in the supermarket were the hard, gassed, pale, and thick-skinned billiard balls provided by the corporate farm to the corporate store. A plastic-wrapped box of mushrooms at the supermarket cost $1.19 a pound; at the Italian market you could buy three pounds of loose mushrooms for $2.00. So it went, all through the list. On the twenty-two items, the Italian market's prices ranged from 7 to 750 percent lower than the supermarket's prices for those same items. If a shopper had bought one unit of everything on that list, he would have paid $20.35 at the city's cheapest supermarket, but only $12.12 for those same items at the Italian market — a saving of $8.23, or roughly 40 percent.

Attracted by the smell of the spice shop, I entered it, and there made another comparison. The shop sold loose bay leaves for fourteen cents an ounce. The price of an ounce of bay leaves, sold in little ⅛-ounce bottles from the supermarket's spice rack, was $6.28.

The fact that bay leaves were sold loose reminded me of something else: just as in Europe, almost everything in the Italian market was sold loose or was only minimally wrapped. The shoppers, as in Europe, carried shopping bags or market baskets into which they put their unwrapped purchases. In the supermarket the foods came wrapped not only once, but often twice, as, for example, tomatoes placed on a plastic tray and covered with a transparent plastic, and bread sheathed in two wrappers. All of these wrapped foods were then placed in double Kraft paper bags. It has been estimated that, as a result of our habit of wrapping everything sold, we Americans throw away in one day more paper, plastic, and foil than Europeans use in one year — and my own experience of having kept house in France, Italy, and England leads me to believe that estimate is correct. In any event, to wrap something in anything costs more than not wrapping it at all, and so when we buy wrapped food we pay for the wrapper as well as the food. And much of the wrapping we do is entirely unnecessary, while some of it is deceitful, as in the case of meats put on plastic trays and sealed in transparent plastic so as to conceal the fact that the side of the meat lying on the opaque tray is chiefly bone or fat. These thoughts led me to price the large plastic bags we put our trash in. What is the price we pay to wrap our unnecessary and expensive trash? Ten large plastic trash bags at the supermarket cost $1.65, whereas ten of the same bags cost $1.18 at the Italian market. An inference here is that the supermarket may be able to charge more for its trash bags because more of its customers have a greater need of them.

The virtues of Philadelphia's Italian market were that its prices were lower, item for item, than the prices of the same items at that city's cheapest supermarket; that the many small shops, stands, and carts lining the five city blocks offered a vastly larger variety of foodstuffs than the supermarket did; and that many of its foodstuffs were fresher, having been locally grown. There were, however, differences in appearance. While all the produce in the supermarket bins was of uniform appearance, as, for example, all the grapefruit being very nearly identical in size and all of them equally round, this was by no means true in the open-air market. But appearance is one thing, and quality is something else. Two ripe Indian River grapefruit may be of precisely the same quality no matter that one of them is round while the other is oblate.

There is no question that the open-air Italian market in Philadelphia offers shoppers a defensive alternative to shopping in the city's supermarkets if price is to be the controlling factor. Convenience is another matter. If the people in the lower-middle-class neighborhood were to give up walking to their nearby supermarket, and shop in the Italian one, they would have to drive eight miles through city traffic to the market, and then try to find parking space in either of the two small and not free parking lots near it or on the crowded, narrow side streets of the neighborhood. They would next have to take the time to walk among the slow throngs on the sidewalks to inspect the offerings in five blocks of shops, stands, and carts to select their purchases. They could buy in an hour at their neighborhood supermarket what could take them an entire morning to buy at the Italian market, and save themselves the ordinary frustrations of city driving and parking and the price of sixteen miles' worth of gasoline. By shopping at the open-air market they could very well save themselves ten dollars a week if not more, and buy much better foods into the bargain, but they would have to be willing to make the effort and find the time.

Many of the reasons why the Italian market is consistently able to undersell the cheapest Philadelphia supermarket have to do with the difference in cost of doing business. The people who man the shops and sidewalk stands are the owners of their businesses and members of their families. There are no clerical staffs, no checkout counter operators, and no cost of union labor at outdoor stalls or in the tiny shops. There are no light, heat, or power bills to pay on a vegetable stand on a sidewalk. The light is provided by the sun, and the heat in winter is provided by a fire built in the street out of boards broken from food crates. The people who own the sidewalk stalls and the shops behind them have been in business for generations, and they have by use and custom (although not at law) acquired the right to use the public street as their rent-free place of business. Much of the produce they sell comes in season from land these families own and garden in New Jersey; many of the fish are sold by those who caught them. The shopkeepers otherwise buy mixed lots of food from farmers as far away as Florida and California; food that, because of its appearance, is not bought by the supermarkets — but that is by no means inferior in quality. It will be remembered that the government's Grade A for produce relates only to appearance and that in America appearance relates to price.

Considering a vendor's ability to do business on a public sidewalk rather than in a heated, lighted, rented, and taxed store staffed by expensive employees, one could see how in many cases the vendor should be able to undersell a supermarket. But each vendor's business is a quite small one, while the supermarket's business is a huge one. And in popular theory, the supermarket should be able to make its money by running a cut-rate business on tremendous volume. In popular theory, the supermarket should be able to undersell anybody. In Philadelphia, the discrepancies between supermarket prices and the Italian market prices were in all cases so large as to suggest that the supermarket prices were suspiciously bloated — and that the reason for this was, as the supermarket spokesman said, that people will pay the price.

The existence of Philadelphia's large open-air market is proof that such an operation is economically viable in a huge city. It has been a going concern for generations. Its success demonstrates that small shops can offer the general public a greater variety of better foods at lower prices than supermarkets do. But the existence of the Philadelphia Italian market is predicated upon the willingness of a few families to be content with modest gain from one generation to the next, spending their lives standing outdoors in all weathers, selling produce. And that is not precisely characteristic of the advertised American dream. Be that as it may, one fact is terribly clear: the existence of this open-air market is the living proof that the supermarket need not be the principal, or only, provision merchant to our civic multitudes. Indeed, a city needs no supermarkets at all. Until a few years ago, there were no supermarkets, although there have been cities for thousands of years.

Please Pass
the Guilt

The New Vegetarians

In the 1960s, when children were burning down the colleges of their choice, a steadily increasing number of people began to give serious thought to food, and concluded that the best thing to do was not to buy it. That is, not to buy the usual foods sold at the usual stores. Their misgivings were prompted, in part, by those who were reporting upon the possibly harmful effects of the chemicals being used by the food industry. Their alternative was to seek out what they called organic, or whole, or natural foods. By these terms, and organic was the one most often used, they meant food that was grown and marketed without the aid of synthetic fertilizers, pesticides, and chemical additives. In short, they wanted to eat the kind of food that people had been eating for thousands of years right up to Grandpa's time: food grown naturally, and if fertilized, then fertilized with manure.

At about the same time, there was an enthusiasm for all

things Oriental, particularly among the young intellectuals. Some young people seemed to imagine that all Orientals are vegetarians who somehow live more spiritual lives than anyone else. The circles of the organic-food seekers often overlapped with the circles of the Orientophiles, as may be seen in this letter from a college student:

> I try to carefully judge the foods I eat not only from the standpoint of what the consequences would be to my physical well-being, but also the far-reaching effects on the world and my spirit. I ask what kind of people produced this food and for what reason. If the food was produced by chemical agribusiness, processed and refined and packaged by a multitude of middlemen, all out to make blood money, is this as good a food as that grown with love and in harmony with nature? No, I don't think it is. So I would prefer those foods that are whole, organic, or natural, purchased as directly as possible from the producer. By buying such foods I would be supporting the small farmer versus the large business monopolies . . . My diet is patterned after the Oriental practice of macrobiotics. Macrobiotics means: encompassing the whole of life. Therefore I eat mostly whole foods [not processed or refined ones], I trust Nature with my body, not a businessman.

The young man's letter went on to describe his diet of grains, fruits, vegetables, and seaweed; it discussed his aversion to killing our brothers, the animals, and stated his belief in eating only in season that which grew naturally in his area.

His letter also indicated the presence of still a third, and overlapping, circle: the vegetarians. In addition to the classic vegetarian, whose diet is his statement of opposition to the slaughter of animals, there are now people I shall call the New Vegetarians, whose reasons are more complex. They include people who think we eat too much meat, people who simply say that meat costs too much, people who believe that a vegetarian diet is the most healthful one, and people who are looking for escapes from what they believe to be a restrictive society. One of the New Vegetarians is Frances Moore Lappé, author of *Diet for a Small Planet*, who frankly admits in her book that her advocacy of a meatless diet appeals "more to my feelings than my rationality.

"First," she writes, "it has to do with the tremendous personal satisfaction of being able to make real choices; indeed, how rare this is! Previously, when I went to a supermarket, I felt at the mercy of our advertising culture. My tastes were manipulated. And food, instead of being my most direct link with the nurturing earth, had become mere merchandising by which I fulfilled my role as a 'good' consumer." *

In another place she writes of discovering that "when a meal was no longer rigidly defined as meat-vegetable-potatoes, many new and exciting culinary experiences became possible." Her basic objection was therefore not to meat, but rather to being a manipulated cipher. Nor did she write her book with an intention to save the world, but rather to point out her discovery of a path to personal salvation.

"The notion of suddenly changing lifelong habits of any kind on the basis of new understanding does not strike me as very realistic or even desirable (however great the revelation!)," she wrote. "At least this is not the way it has worked in my family . . . Never did we swear off meat, vowing to make this a great sacrifice for the sake of mankind! Rather, meat began to play a smaller and smaller role in our diet as it was displaced by new and, frankly, more interesting ways of meeting our daily protein need."

Nevertheless, Mrs. Lappé did raise the grain-beef argument that is used by other New Vegetarians who *do* want to

* Ballantine Books, New York, 1971.

save the world, and here we come to still a fourth circle, which often overlaps with the others.

The argument is that it takes seven to eight pounds of grain to produce a pound of beef. With hunger and malnutrition chronic in the Third World, it is sinful to feed all that protein-rich grain to beef cattle. We should not fatten cattle on grain, but send that grain to the starving. If we ate less meat, or no meat, we would have more grain to send abroad. To this argument there is usually appended the statement that the world is running out of food as the world's population continues to explode.

The argument is specious and the statement may be false. Cattle can be, and in many places are, raised entirely on forage that cannot be eaten by people and that grows on land that cannot support grain. It is quite possible to have both cattle *and* grain; there is no necessary one-to-one relationship. Then, according to the May 1975 issue of *Science* magazine, the world's food supply is adequate and is increasing at a faster rate than the population is exploding. Be this as it may, the important thing is that many of the New Vegetarians believe in both the argument and the statement, and use both to recruit adherents to their humanitarian concern for the Third World.

After reviewing their positions, I have concluded that there is one thing, and only one thing, that all the critics of the food industry, all the organic food enthusiasts, all the Orientophiles, and all the New Vegetarians and concerned humanitarians have in common. It is their dissatisfaction with the modern American way of life. They are all saying there is something wrong with the way we live, something wrong with what we do, much that is wrong with what the supermarkets offer us. They are saying we must live and behave quite differently, for the sake of mankind as well as for the sake of our own bodies and souls, and that we can begin to change for the better by changing our attitude toward food. We are, in effect, being asked to embrace a religion that, like many another, observes dietary laws.

A great many of the new religionists are college students and young married people. Most of them are white, suburban, and affluent; unlike early Christianity, the new religion is a middle-class enthusiasm. Not a few of them seem to find something reprehensible about being white, suburban, affluent, or even American. All of them in any case strike me as being disappointed by America and as being the advocates of change. Since people seldom have one reason for doing whatever they do, I have wondered what other reasons, apart from those they set forth, they might have for their disaffections and feelings of guilt. I suggest, purely speculatively, that our having dropped two atomic bombs upon a prostrate Japan might have something to do with their attitude; that the intellectual insults of advertising, the inanity of television, the silliness and moral depravity of Watergate, the commercial pollution of our air, land, and water, and a hundred other disappointing aspects of American life, including twenty years of pointless warfare in Asia, might all lie deeply beneath their attitude toward the American food industry, which they subconsciously see as a construct of what President Eisenhower called the military-industrial complex. It seems to me they are not merely saying No to the food in the supermarket, but that they are essentially saying No to the society that produced it, whether they are aware of this or not.

In the early 1960s, the number of the disaffected seemed as small as that cloud upon the horizon that was no larger than a man's hand. But as the news worsened, the number increased. So did the number of health food stores, and so did the prices charged in those stores, where people were soon paying more than beef prices for their buckwheat groats, brown rice, and sunflower seeds.

The production of organic foods increased, and shops that

sold only organic foods appeared. In little more than a decade, the production of organic food climbed from near zero to a $500-million-a-year business. This seems an impressive number, and indeed it is — not because it is large, but rather because the rate of growth is portentous. When compared with the more than $160-billion-a-year corporate food business, the organic food business is statistically insignificant. So too is the acreage. When compared with the vast reaches of corporate farmlands, the land given to organic farming is the smallest of gardens — a comparative windowbox. But the rate of growth is impressive, and the people most impressed by it are those in the food industry, whose first reaction could most charitably be described as hysterical.

Earl Butz, United States Secretary of Agriculture, wanted to strangle this creature at birth. Mr. Butz, who is regarded by his critics as being a creature of the food industry, was reported as saying that if organic farming methods were generally adopted, this would mean starvation for fifty million Americans. The Agriculture Department sent officials to San Francisco in 1974 to address a panel, loaded with food industry personnel, on the subject "The Food Supply and the Organic Food Myth." To members of the food industry, anyone who wanted to eat unprocessed food that was naturally grown was nothing in the world but a long-haired, hippie food freak who was dangerous to the peace and good order of the United States of America because he was getting people all upset. Dr. Thomas H. Jukes, for twenty years a research chemist at American Cyanamid, warned that a fellow like that "brings about a mistrust of the present food supply."

If the Agriculture Department and the food industry's reaction was rather like that of a man using a howitzer to kill a gnat, it must be borne in mind that the gnat was, and is, dangerous. If the organic food movement continues to grow as it has been growing, the food industry stands to lose more than the $500 million it has already lost to organic foods.

The industry's second reaction was much more sophisticated. It was to pre-empt the health food and organic food market for itself. The industry entered what it called, with unconscious irony, the "good food" market. Televised pictures of rural scenes were created, with good old Grandpas and good old Grannys smiling, and with pictures of wonderful raw foods, like honey and golden grain, that became good old bread, these pictures being shown while good old music, like "My Old Kentucky Home," played in the background. Using brand names like Nature Valley and Country Morning, the cereal people were going to give us just good old natural 100 percent grain with nothing added — except of course a ton of sugar and a higher price.

It is altogether unreasonable to believe that the food industry, which is entirely predicated upon the unnatural production of unnatural foods, can actually be producing organic ones. It is easier to believe the industry is once again creating illusions while hiking prices, meanwhile depending on the theory that the general public is silly enough to believe its advertisements. If this is so, no doubt some people would think it clever of the food industry to pretend to fall in with an emergent popular longing for the honest foods of yesteryear, and by pretense seal off a potentially dangerous threat to corporate profits.

Both in their first hysterical response to organic foods, and next in their sophisticated one, the industrialists exhibited a singular concern for public opinion. One is tempted to say that only the guilty could feel so frightened. Another view could be that, as a manipulator of public opinion, the industry understands that the public can be manipulated, and is constantly worried that somebody else might do the manipulating. A widening public concern for purity in foods and for nutritive value is an apparent fact, and responding to this fact, the food industry wishes to appear as the very champion of purity and value.

At the same time, the industry also wishes to appear as endlessly innovative in the public interest, ever searching for ways of producing even better foods — and this leads us to the curious world of New Foods. Picking up on what they hear in the public air, the New Food section of the food industry forthrightly stands for nutrition, for vegetarianism, for saving the world from famine as the population increases, for lower prices for everyone, for a new way of life, and for less work for Mother. All these good causes and purposes are served by science, the New Food people say, because science can produce much better food than Nature can. Cutting all the ground out from under the organic food enthusiasts with the speed of light, while in the same split second seeming to agree with their disaffection and to use all their arguments, the New Food people promise new foods for a new world — and this matter is so novel that I think it appropriate for us to turn to a new topic.

The Ten-Foot Egg

I have seen the future, and I am afraid it is going to work. We shall, in the space of another generation, have massfood for massman, untouched by human hands from seed bed to dining room table. All the processes, from seeding to cultivation to harvest to packaging to transportation to supermarket, will be performed mechanically, and at the checkout counter your bank account will be electronically debited while the store's account will be simultaneously credited.

It is a future in which laser-directed mechanical moles till
the fields; in which unmanned helicopters or Hovercraft
mechanically perform all the weeding, fertilizing, spraying,
and tending once done by man. Sound waves will tell a
computer when the fruit is ripe, and the computer will
instantly transmit an electrical impulse to break the twigs to
drop the ripe fruit on to a soft, endlessly moving belt below,
which will carry the fruit to the completely automated
packaging plant from which the packages will be automatically loaded aboard supersonic transports.

The farmers of the future may be an office staff of men or
women who work consecutive eight-hour shifts in a building
like the Houston space center, two thousand miles away from
the fields and orchards they tend. They can sit before
consoles, watching lines and blips of light flicker on television screens; they can read teleprintouts, push buttons, and
thereby monitor all the circuits that hatch, raise, feed,
slaughter, dress, package, ship, and sell chickens; they can
simultaneously raise, feed, slaughter, box, and ship cattle
— and meanwhile raise enough soybeans to feed the Orient,
Ultima Thule, and all the astronauts in all the space stations
in orbit.

There is even now an unmanned satellite in orbit, watching over all the earth's growing things with its godlike
electronic eyes, distinguishing among various kinds of vege-
tation, detecting insect infestations, monitoring the effective-
ness of wind erosion controls, using space data in watershed
hydrology. The satellite is called ERTS-1, meaning the first
Earth Resources Technology Satellite, and it was launched
on July 23, 1972, by the National Aeronautics and Space
Administration. The remote-sensing apparatus aboard the
spacecraft is linked to ground-based computers that convert
its signals into tapes that, according to the United States
Department of Agriculture, "identify and measure land use;

detect plant diseases, insect infestation and drought; assess crop stands and predict future yields; determine whether soils are suitable for growing needed crops."

By simple elaboration on existing technology, such a satellite could see to it that timely deliveries of adequate amounts of foodstuffs are automatically dispatched to their appropriate destinations anywhere on earth. The satellite is operational now, and so are the laser-directed moles, the electrically dropped-by-remote-control ripe fruit, and all the other devices mentioned above. You may call it science if you will, but you cannot call it fiction. The future is hurtling upon us as fast as money can hurry it, and the Department of Agriculture looks upon this brave new world and finds it good.

"Mechanization comes, traditions go," the department says in its illustrated publication, *Science for Living*, whose logotype is set in computer lettering.* "Mechanization can save an industry that might not survive labor scarcity. It conserves manpower by making better jobs — jobs that call for higher skills and higher pay. A new farm machine creates jobs for the men who build it, and brings economic prosperity to a community. Mechanization has saved more than three billion man hours of farm labor over the past fifteen years. During the same time, production of crops went up twenty-two percent."

I find this sort of logic endlessly fascinating. Mechanization has not "saved" three billion man hours of farm labor; it has saved corporate growers three billion pay-roll hours, which is to say it has subtracted three billion hours from farm laborers' paychecks. If the agriculture industry finds itself a bit short-handed, a reason for this is that it has been tractoring people off the land. Apparently, further mechanization is now needed to chase the rest of them away — and the Department of Agriculture just as apparently thinks this

* Agriculture Information Bulletin No. 363, January 1974.

would be a fine idea, for its bulletin also says, "Today's research engineers *can look ahead from this vantage point* to visualize the future as a time *when all the work on the farm* is carried out by automated machinery, directed by tape-controlled programs, and supervised by television scanners mounted on towers." (Italics added.)

What increasingly sophisticated mechanization of farming will do, and what in fact it is actually designed to do, is to throw people out of work in order that the grower can save money. Over and again the department's bulletin speaks in terms of saving labor costs. In the case of automatically harvested grapefruit, for instance, the bulletin happily reports, "Harvest cost is estimated to 15 cents per field box — *9 cents a box less than the break-even cost of hand-picking.*" (Italics added.)

To be sure, the invention of a new farm machine could create jobs for the people who build it, but, since the intended effect of the machine is to take jobs away from a great many more people, it is difficult to see how this "brings economic prosperity to a community." Manpower could certainly be conserved if none were needed, but what do the men do whose power is being conserved? What are the "better jobs" that await them if, as the Agriculture Department supposes, such jobs require higher skills than they now possess?

I do not wish to seem a latter-day Luddite; I merely feel that the purpose of a machine ought to be to enable a man to do whatever he does more easily — its purpose should not be to dispense with the man entirely. Automation in many industries around the world has already created acute social problems, and in England one group of research engineers is now devoting *its* efforts to inventing farm machines and factory techniques that, instead of replacing people, will enable more people to be employed at less onerous and more interesting hand labor.

In America, however, everywhere you go in the food industry you meet the grinning face of science, not that of humanity, and it is the face of a science that is single-mindedly devoted to lowering costs and dispensing with human labor while increasing production and profits.

The scientists call themselves food engineers, and food engineering is a term that embraces not only all that pertains to growing, processing, packaging, transporting, and marketing foodstuffs, but also the invention of entirely new foods (such as wholly synthetic cheeses, ten-foot-long hardboiled eggs, fake sausage the length of a garden hose, and all manner of fake meats, poultry, and fish made from soybeans, together with fastfood snacks made out of cotton) and plaster walls made out of chicken blood.

These scientists are the New Food men, and they collectively resemble in manner, confidence, and appearance the kind of men President Nixon employed in the White House. They all seem to have that same eager-beaver look; they are full of numbers and earnest conviction; they bounce with health and business; they are the intelligent products of the incomplete education offered in our state universities — having apparently opted for all the courses in the catalogue except the humanities.

One of them was a Department of Agriculture research scientist who assured me that in fifty years there will be fake steak for everyone, and butchers will be as rare as fletchers.

"Oh," he said, "I suppose there will always be a few people, a few rich people, who will still want genuine things, but everyone else here and around the world will be eating meat analogs that look and taste and smell and have the same texture as steak, and are just as nutritious if not more so."

The scientist's presumption that only the rich desire the genuine was typical of his swift judgments upon his fellow man.

"In this time-frame," he said, "we need a total escalation of flexible response in order to minimize counterproductive waste levels. And we'll have to quantify that."

Asked to translate this, he provided an example:

"Why grow a hundred pounds of grain to get ten pounds of beef when you can eat the hundred pounds of grain yourself, if it's engineered into fake steak and nobody can tell the difference?"

This was not precisely the grain-beef argument of the New Vegetarians, because the New Food scientist was interested in profits, not in people.

"You can cut the production cost of steak by seventy-five percent if you make it out of beans instead of beef. So who needs cattle?"

When New Food men raise their eyes abroad, they see a lot of hungry customers out there. "The profit-study picture makes the case for more foreign ventures," one of them said. "And one of the benefits we get from big outfits like General Foods is that the big multinationals are more able than anybody else to solve world food problems. They'll tell you this at the Harvard Business School: engineered foods are the hottest invention since fire, and if you want to make money, you better get into engineered foods right away."

In their conversations with the public, however, the New Food men do borrow the grain-beef argument. "It's going to get to the point where the world won't be able to produce enough natural food to feed its people," one manufacturer's representative told a press conference. "You've got to consider how many pounds of meat will be available per capita by the turn of the century. Imitation food, the ability of food technologists to duplicate Nature, may be the key to the future. We can now go Him one better."

Then, plucking chords familiar not only to the New Vegetarians but also to anyone else who reads newspapers, magazines, or RDA labels, he bore down heavily on the nutritional value of bogus meat made from textured vegetable protein, known in the trade as TVP. The vegetable in this case was the soybean. His TVP steaks, he said, had no fat, no cholesterol, very few calories, and were just as nutritious as real meat, if not more so. True, no one on a low salt diet should eat them, but for anyone else the nutritional value was incontestable. But more important, or so it seemed to his audience, was the low cost. There was little shrinkage, no waste, and the product had a long shelf-life providing it was kept frozen. In sum, here was a TVP fake steak, with or without optional fake grill markings, that could cost the housewife as little as nine cents a serving, that would be just as tasty and just as good as the porterhouse at sixty cents a serving.

"Now here's a cute thing," a New Food engineer said. "You can make a ten-foot egg or a mile-long salami. Who wants one? Why, my God! Resaurants want one! Suppose you were working in a restaurant and you were slicing up hardboiled eggs for chicken salads. Wouldn't you rather slice up a ten-foot egg than slice up ten feet worth of individual hardboiled eggs? Think of the saving in labor costs! And every slice is like a center slice. The white looks and tastes like white, the yolk looks and tastes like yolk, you can serve this egg hot, cold, sliced, diced, whatever you want. Just like egg, but no cholesterol — and no goddamn shells! Plus, at today's egg prices, you can buy enough fake egg to make nine hundred slices, for thirty-nine dollars and three cents less than you could buy enough real eggs to make nine hundred slices — and if you bought real eggs, not every slice would be a center slice. Plus no spoilage, no breakage. Costwise and pricewise, it's beautiful! You might do even better on a mile of salami."

It is not just fake steak, fake egg, or fake salami. There is also a false cheese, which its manufacturer calls "a totally positive product" that comes in "American or mozzarella flavors. All the goodness of natural cheese without all the cost." Another manufacturer takes a high-protein, low-cholesterol soybean extract, which is then curdled with acid, washed, dissolved, spun, bleached, woven, rolled, pumped into a tube, injected with synthetic ham flavoring and coloring, vibrated, heated, and — Voila! Ham! It's the only ham in the world, the manufacturer's representative somewhat proudly said, that can be served in a kosher restaurant.

"When we make a food," another New Food man said, "whether it's chicken, ham, scallops, or lobster, we give it a certain flavor and texture and appearance, and that's the way it stays as long as it's frozen, and you'll never be able to tell the difference between it and the real thing."

"At first we did want to hide the fact that our 'meats' weren't really meats at all, but imitations," a General Mills spokesman told a reporter. "But now we prefer that our consumers know just what it is they're eating. There should be no deception whatsoever on anybody's part. The halo that has been held over real meat products has become very rusty — real meat just isn't as sacred as it used to be. And if a restaurant owner is going to serve a meat replacer, he should hold his head high. If he's going to claim it's real meat, though, he should be thrown in jail."

Other manufacturers are not so scrupulous, at least not in their advertising in food industry trade journals. Miles Laboratories, the manufacturer of Alka Seltzer (among other products), produces TVP extenders and analogs that provide "a high quality flexible alternative for meat and seafood"; this alternative "retain[s] . . . texture, color and mouthfeel all the way through cooking, canning, freezing and thawing, right to your customer's table." Its Seapro, for example, was "formulated especially for use with seafoods. Seapro blends exceedingly well (at up to 50% levels) with crab meat, tuna, lobster, fish, or shrimp. Actually can improve the texture of products made with these seafoods, yet reduce costs significantly. Because Seapro is a spun vegetable protein, it can be ground, cubed, chopped or flaked to duplicate your seafood ingredients."

"What did you say the name of this outfit was?" asked the director of a Pennsylvania restaurant association. "How come they've been keeping this a secret, and where can I find these guys? That's a wonderful idea."

While visions of selling soybeans at lobster prices danced in the fellow's head, millions of us have already been paying hot dog prices for soybeans whenever we have bought frankfurters at baseball parks, airports, and fastfood snack-stands that purchase their weiners from Automatic Retailers of America, Inc., a concern that does a nationwide business. ARA's director of their Research and Standards Department says their products meet Department of Agriculture school lunch requirements, which permit the use of 30 percent TVP in meats, and that their products are clearly labeled, as required by the Food and Drug Administration. The people who buy ARA hot dogs by the case therefore know what they are buying — but not necessarily the fellow in the white suit who sells them in the stadium, or the people who eat them.

If you have eaten a public school lunch or dined in a government cafeteria or in a hospital, you have probably eaten meat extended with TVP. Whether you have paid lobster or beef prices for soybeans at your favorite restaurant is something known only to the proprietor. Much as the General Mills spokesman might say, when talking to the press, that such a cheat should be thrown in jail, no such point was raised at a hotel-motel-restaurant trade convention, where General Mills was peddling its Bontrae line of

TVP beef, ham, and chicken on the premise that its products were "economical, convenient, USDA-approved, flavorful, appetizing, and pre-cooked."

When you buy fake meat, clearly labeled as such, at your friendly neighborhood supermarket, not all of the savings in cost between the bogus and genuine will be passed along to you — although they will certainly be realized by the manufacturer and the supermarket. Miles Laboratories test-marketed its line of Morningstar Farms breakfast sausages and bacon, made of soybeans, in Chicago and on the West Coast at real meat prices. The company was happily surprised to find their products outselling the natural equivalents. The strong selling point is the fact that these ersatz meats contain no cholesterol, no animal fat; people were apparently willing to pay for this. The test results certainly did not suggest that Miles Laboratories should rush to lower its prices. Lloyd Slater, editor of *Food Engineering*, guessed that "prices may come down years from now," but he said that New Food was a young industry that would "have to keep its prices up until it really gets going." He was meanwhile amused by the Morningstar Farms brand name, with its implication that a product made in a chemical works was a farm-fresh food. "Well," he said as he grinned, "soybeans grow on farms, don't they?"

The New Food industry might be a young one, but it was born with a golden spoon in its mouth, for the corporations investing in it include several of the world's largest, richest multinational conglomerates. While great emphasis is being put on the soybean as a source of protein that can be made to resemble meat, research proceeds on other possible sources, such as cottonseed and yeasts. The Soviet Union already has four factories busily turning out proteins from yeast grown on petroleum substrates. Petrochemicals are expensive, but this apparently does not bother the Russians, who have plenty of oil of their own. The yeast is collected, dried, and then, by chemical and mechanical means, is engineered into a food fed to livestock. The Russians' next step is to engineer it into something that can be fed directly to people. The American Oil Company is conducting its own experiments with yeast grown on petroleum substrates; they can be grown in filling station grease pits, or on the outfall from pulp mills, or on piles of garbage. Then, like TVP, they can be engineered into a simulacrum of almost any food anyone is imaginative enough to imitate. One need not merely imitate meat, eggs, or cheese and fish; one can also manufacture apples that are not apples, okra that is not okra, melons that are not melons. Beyond this lies a second generation of New Food: wholly synthetic foods that are analogous to nothing on earth — foods with flavors and textures as yet unknown. Mr. Slater, for one, hopes he'll live to see the day. "There's a lot of promise in creative foods," he said.

Research is also proceeding in the realm of real food — particularly in genetics. Chickens have been crossed with turkeys and pheasants, pheasants with turkeys, and turkeys and chickens with quail. The possibilities seem endless, including perhaps the wren with the emu. The featherless chicken is almost, but not quite, a bird in hand; some way will have to be found to prevent the recently developed featherless chicken from dying of pneumonia. Geneticists have also come up with sheep that breed year round, not just in the fall; they have devised a way of bringing about multiple births in sheep and cattle. Another experiment has proved successful: if you feed a sheep cyclophosphamide, you can fire your wool shearers, because the chemical causes the whole fleece to separate at the skinline, so instead of having to shear the beast, you simply grab it by the back of the neck, give the fleece a yank, and it all comes off in one piece, leaving the sheep nude and shivering. Then, reaching back into the past, geneticists have produced the beefalo — a cross between the American bison and beef cattle. Like the buffalo, it is high in protein, low on fat, can snuffle under the snow in winter to feed on buffalo grass, and reaches maturity sooner than beef cattle. At the same time, it is easier to manage than a buffalo and requires much less attention than cattle. If the beefalo rather than the soybean should be the steak of the future, many cowboys will have to start looking for another line of work — because here, as elsewhere in food engineering, we enter (as Smollett said of marriage) the state of wholly matter-money.

Money is what all of this is really all about. The fully automated farm serves no real purpose in God's green world except to save its owner the expense of hiring people. The giant multinational conglomerates are not pouring millions into the New Food industry for reasons of philanthropy; to provide more nourishment; to feed a hungry world. They are in the business to make money out of it, and this is the reason why chicken farmers are praying for the development of a featherless chicken that won't catch cold. The arguments for New Food are largely deceptive. A fake meat might in one sense be as or even more nutritious than a natural one, but in another sense it well might not, because not all the additives necessary to imitate flavor and texture may be beneficial to everyone. When New Food people assure us that "you can't taste the difference" between a soybean breakfast sausage and the real thing, they can only have in mind those with tastebuds of synthetic rubber, or, more likely, they have in mind driving the nation's pig farmers out of business and winning a billion dollar market for themselves. There is no reason for New Food other than economic advantage. No one has demanded New Food; no one needs it. The only reason it exists is that when a New Food engineer stares into the future and sees America thickly carpeted with soybeans from sea to shining sea, with television scanners monitoring the crop, and machines tending it, and automated factories turning out fake meat, cheese, fruit, vegetables, fish, salad, and desserts, he sees green.

God may be called in to play a part. He was, recently, in Jamestown, Ohio, where a church group set out two plots of soybeans. The faithful prayed for the beans in one plot, and did not pray for the beans in the other. The prayed-for beans provided a 4 percent higher yield, thus proving, to the satisfaction of Gus Alexander, doctor of communications at Wright State University, that "somehow God's creative energy of growth can be channeled through us even to plants. If put to use, our psychic abilities — our abilities of prayer — could vastly improve the world's food supply. By some means, when a person concentrates on sending his love, God channels that love to others, to a pet or even a plot of soybeans. In this case, it's healing for the soybeans."

OK, God, that's it. You've done Your part. Thanks a lot. We'll take it from there and turn those soybeans into a heap better and different stuff from what You planted in the Garden. We have a new line of bees now, God. They're bred so they fly only to bean flowers, and make a beeline back to the plastic honeycombs we've set up for them. We have a project going to make the honeycomb edible. Otherwise, we're in good shape. See You around, God, when it's time for the helicopters to set out the next bean crop . . . Right now we have to go to the temple to see the money-changers . . .

The temple, by the way, is becoming increasingly computerized and electrified. "The consumer of tomorrow," the Agriculture Department says, "will probably go to a push-button supermarket. There he will drop a coded card into a slot beside the commodity selected and punch a button.

Impulses travel two ways — to a cash register where the bill is totaled, and to a central warehouse where the order is assembled. The completed order will await the customer at his car." Already there are computerized supermarkets where clerks with electronic scanners point the scanners at the coded labels, the small discs or oblongs of black lines you see on many cans and other packages. The scanners read the code and send the message to the computer, which identifies the product and its current price, activates a machine that prints out your shopping list and bill, and simultaneously keeps a running account of sales and inventory levels for the store. This, in the future, will be keyed into the electronic bank account, so that your account will be automatically debited and the store's account credited, and no one will have to use money. Such bank-store-customer arrangements are also a contemporary reality, past the purely theoretical and testing stages, and when they are hooked into the clerkless push-button supermarket the Agriculture Department envisions, then the circle will be complete. Then no one will raise, reap, package, ship, or even sell food. Instead, machines will do all of this, and all the food will be fake.

In the event that there may still be a few genuine people left in the world who might desire genuine things, I should like to take a genuine and reasonably athletic child into one of those completely automated push-button supermarkets of the future and tell the little fellow to push all the buttons he can reach, as often as he wishes, and watch him run happily about, pushing buttons, and see a mountain of packages of fake food automatically rising and spilling and piling up on the curb, burying the motorcars, while the automated cash register goes ding ding ding ding as the happy child laughs and pushes button after button. Such opportunities to have a bit of genuine fun might be only too rare in the kind of world the New Food people wish to press on us.

In fairness to the New Food engineers, I think we might pray, "Have mercy on them, Lord, for they know not what they do. The Golden Calf they worship is textured vegetable protein and just as fake as one of their soybean steaks with the optional grill markings."

It is difficult, however, to be fair when one is in danger of losing one's life. The danger that the New Food engineers pose is that the uses of science are being marshaled by enormously wealthy and powerful industries, perhaps unwittingly but nonetheless certainly, to drive out the genuine in favor of the false — not in the service of man, but rather in service to themselves, for the greater glory of Mammon.

Eating Out
for a Change

How Doggy Is Your Bag, Dad?

The Old Stone Goose is a restaurant ten miles from the city, in a suburban township. It is a thing of wagon wheels, electric lanterns, huge black cauldrons on the lawn, with parking lot attendants in Colonial regimentals. Inside are low ceilings with polished copper pots hanging from beams, and two dark bars that are always filled with people noisily filling themselves as they wait for tables.

Our host gave his name to an elf wearing a ruffled shirt, huge bow tie, purple trousers, and a dinner jacket of many shimmering colors. We followed his long blond hair on a kind of eel-dance along a crowded corridor to a dining room, eeling through the close-together tables and the nearly touching chairs to the table that had been reserved for us in a corner beneath an air conditioner.

A waitress in a white mob cap, her bosom, a somewhat aging one, bubbling out of a low-cut and miniskirted version of a Puritan gown, poured ice water into our tumblers, asked what we wanted to drink, and handed us menus the size of the Sunday *New York Times.*

Our dining room was one of three in The Old Stone Goose. All were as crowded as the Stygian bars and the corridors, and we did not talk. Instead, we leaned close when we saw someone's mouth opening and closing, and shouted fragments of speech into whatever spaces could be found in the general uproar.

". . . here before?"

"No, I . . ."

". . . teen miles a gallon."

". . . measles, but I think . . ."

From time to time an electronically magnified voice brayed throughout the establishment. Would the owner of the dark red Oldsmobile with New Jersey plates please come to the desk, he had left his car locked in the driveway?

"You made up your minds yet?" our waitress demanded, her voice, like that of the loudspeaker, a file especially adapted to rasp through the din. She handed around the whiskey sours and vodka martinis our host had ordered.

We guiltily sought to compose our absent minds, trying to hold the menus so as not to poke their corners into the eyes of neighboring diners, while the waitress set upon the tiny table a two-feet-high peppermill, wooden bowls of green salads, a breadboard with a knife and a small loaf of hot bread on it, a lazy Susan of bird baths containing applesauce, cottage cheese, and watermelon rind pickles, and a bowl sprinkled with congealed pats of butter sliding around on melting ice cubes.

"French, Russian, or blue?" the waitress demanded, complicating our struggles with the menus as she elbowed among us to ladle thick sauces onto the dry, brown-edged shreds of leaves. Beneath her miniskirt she wore fishnet pantyhose.

Our host told her he would order when we had our second drinks.

Everything was à la carte. In the median range of prices, one found the Châteaubriand for two at $23.00 and the Princess Filet Mignon, meaning a small one, for $8.75. Three Crisp French Onion Rings could be had for $1.50. The menu indicated our salad was free. It appeared to have been liberated shortly after the Crimean War.

The wine list was brief. Port was listed as a red table wine; sauterne had its place among the whites. God knows what our host must have paid for two rounds of drinks, two bottles of rather sour and certainly spurious Burgundy, dinner for the six of us, and coffee and brandy afterward. It was probably enough to have kept a family of six for a week, including the children's trips to the orthodontist.

The food was neither garbage nor ambrosia; neither British nor French. It really had no character of any kind. It was rather like airline food in that it is difficult to recall. To my mind, the most impressive thing about this festive occasion was that everyone at the bars and in the dining rooms seemed to be having a wonderful time. The Old Stone Goose was running at its noisy capacity when we arrived, and it was just as crowded when we left, with still more Cadillacs inchworming their way into the parking lot. The people in our party all remarked how good the food was, how efficient the service, and how reasonable the price for what you received. One of them said The Old Stone Goose was just about the best place there was around there to eat out, and you absolutely had to have a reservation. My wife and I were a lonely minority; our hearts went out to our host. I was sure that the party guest was right: The Old Stone Goose *was* the best place to eat for miles around. Our host had gone to considerable pains and expense to give us a meal at the best of available restaurants, and I was just as sorry for him as I was irritated by everything about The Old Stone Goose — from its silly pretenses to its unfortunate clientele.

The Old Stone Geese of this nation waddle around

everywhere from New Orleans to Boston; from New York to San Francisco. They are the restaurants of the middle class. Below them are the national chains of fastfood drive-ins; above them are a handful of exquisite restaurants whose prices are as necessarily high as the quality of the cuisine. In between these extremes there are a diminishing number of choices, each of them either more or less Stone Goosey, depending upon which side of the line they lie, a great many of them being foreign or pseudo-foreign, and most of them far too expensive in view of what they purvey. Since the United States government *includes what we spend in restaurants* when it estimates what the American family spends for its food, and since The Old Stone Goose represents a kind of absolute dead center of taste, let us return for a moment to that establishment to find out what we are actually paying for — and how the management can get away with it.

The first thing we pay for is appearance. The Old Stone Goose purports to be an old Colonial inn. If some attempt had been made to re-create such an inn, with meat turning on a spit in the fireplace; with Colonial drink and Colonial fare prepared in accordance with original recipes; with real candlelight provided by hand-dipped candles; with genuine kitchen and table utensils and furniture; then the price of appearance might be justified. What has been created is, however, Walt Disney Colonial, an insult to intelligence. There are hundreds of restaurants in America equally insulting; restaurants wherein you can dine in a jail cell; in the rear seat of a Rolls-Royce; where cowgirls shoot .45 caliber blank cartridges when they bring on slabs of steak; where the whole dining room slowly revolves on the top of a high building; where you eat in Hell with devils in red leotards bringing you food on pitchforks; restaurants where you are served by female rabbits; and others where the requirement is to put on funny hats. Each such appearance, like the ersatz Colonial of The Old Stone Goose, is a travesty of taste, and so, for that matter, is the food.

A second thing we pay for is the bar. The high noise levels of our Old Stone Geese float about on an ocean of alcohol. As the levels in the glasses fall, the higher the sound rises. I have no objection to people drinking; my objection is to people drinking to the point of braying and shouting. It is precisely to this point that they are led by the head ganders of our Stone Geese, who, well aware that the bar makes money, steer the customers into it to await the preparation of the tables. When allowed to emerge, glazed of eye and loud of mouth, they may indeed be having a wonderful time, but their conviviality owes nothing to their anticipation of that old Colonial favorite, Ye Steake Diane, or to their enjoyment of anything else about the restaurant. If we join them in their alcoholic euphoria, we must pay the price of this, and if we do not, then we must pay the price of that. If, by the way, you do have a drink at the bar, you may be surprised to find that what is poured from a bottle of your favorite brand does not taste exactly like your favorite brand. The larger and more anonymous the clientele of an Old Stone Goose, the more probable this sort of surprise.

The third price we pay is that of the food. The menu advertises prime beef. If you ordered the Princess Filet Mignon, no doubt you noticed that it was not filet mignon, and that it more closely resembled U.S. Good than it did U.S. Prime. The Prime Rib of Beef au Jus, at twenty dollars, was huge, tender, and tasty, and it certainly was, or had been, the prime rib of a beef. But it was not a prime rib of a prime beef. Its color was rather strange; it was a uniform rose pink from center to edge. It was so tender it could be cut with a fork; in fact, it seemed to lack the texture of roast beef. It was served au jus, but with an unusually spicy and

rather more than beefy kind of liquid that was reminiscent of
. . . well . . . reminiscent of a melting bouillon cube, come
to think of it. It was also served with canned asparagus. If
your string beans and mushrooms tasted like something you
had encountered elsewhere, the reason you think so might
very well be that you have encountered them elsewhere: at
other Stone Geese and on airline dinner trays. It must be
said we were served a great deal of food, much more than we
wanted to eat; so much more that the waitress asked if we
wanted doggy bags. Nowhere else in the world do restaurants so grossly overfeed their diners; nowhere else in
Christendom do restaurants presume their patrons wish to
scrape their plates and carry their garbage home with them.
Apparently, part of the price we pay at an Old Stone Goose
is that of being taken for, and treated like, a dog.

As for the Prime Filet Mignon that seemed to be neither
prime nor a filet, it is, as Glorio J. Tatsy says, illegal for a
restaurateur to say on his menu that his meat is prime when
in fact it is not. But as Mr. Tatsy also says, in his capacity as
Chief of the Division of Food Control for the State of
Pennsylvania, "There isn't much that we can do about it,
because when we come to press charges, the restaurant
owner will say, 'Gee, *we* thought it was prime beef; that's
what we order; the *supplier* must have made a mistake that
day.'" Mr. Tatsy complained, as all civil servants are wont
to do, of a lack of funds. He said the state did not
appropriate money enough to hire inspectors in numbers
sufficient to keep restaurateurs honest. What is true of
Pennsylvania is true of other jurisdictions in this regard, and
the Prime/Good Switch, as it is called, is a simple ploy that is
universally practiced.

The curious color, texture, and taste of that huge prime rib,
which like the string beans and mushrooms may be found
elsewhere, was perhaps a dyed, tenderized, flavor-added

product. "Because of the rapid advances in food processing and packaging techniques," the Food and Drug Administration says, "all consumers, in a sense, are served from great communal kitchens — the processing plants of national manufacturers." One such manufacturer offers a line of frozen meats "shaped like filets," as he says, which the restaurateur can buy by the case at a price that figures out to seventy-eight cents apiece, and which he might very well call a Princess Filet and serve to you for $8.75. There are seafood houses that sell frozen "shore dinners" or "combination seafood platters" to seafood restaurants. The price per serving that the restaurateur pays for one seafood dish is fourteen cents, and its manufacturer suggests the restaurant ought to be able to sell it for $2.50. Of course there is no requirement that the restaurant do so; any restaurant can charge what it pleases so far as the manufacturer is concerned. There is a central supplier of precooked, honey-batter frozen chicken parts. These are sold to national chains of fingerfood snackstands and to any other restaurant that wishes to advertise its "honey-glazed chicken" as a *spécialité de la maison.*

If much of the food at an Old Stone Goose resembles airline food, this may be because that is exactly what it is. A corporate kitchen in Chicago cooks and freezes "in convenient half size steam table pans," with "English/Spanish heating instructions" on them, the following delicacies: Beef Burgundy, Beef Stroganoff, Stuffed Green Peppers, Macaroni and Cheese, Tuna and Noodles, Beef Stew, Chicken Fricassee, Salisbury Steak with Mushroom Gravy, Salisbury Steak with Onion Gravy, Stuffed Cabbage Rolls, Veal Parmigiana, Turkey à la King, Lasagna with Meat, Swedish Meatballs, Noodles and Chicken, Chicken Chow Mein, and Braised Sirloin Tips. The concern does a nationwide business, supplying our Old Stone Geese with what amounts to frozen TV dinners, which are then purveyed to us at whatever price the restaurant wishes to place upon its Walt Disney Colonial charm. The rule is, the more tricked out the restaurant, the more it is likely to charge for thawing and serving an airline dinner.

Another midwestern manufacturer supplies French foods nationwide. The food is no more French than I am, but let us pass that point for the moment. One result of this manufacturer's enterprise is that the same dish can appear in seventeen different French restaurants in a single city under seventeen different names at seventeen different prices. If you should go to one of those little French restaurants the size of a broom closet and there be handed a menu two pages long, you might wonder how in the world the restaurant could offer so many choices in view of its limited seating capacity and obviously small volume of business. If the restaurateur bought each day the fresh ingredients of all those dishes, then he must have to throw out tremendous amounts of uneaten supplies. The answer is likely to be that very little is fresh; that the restaurateur has only to open his deepest freeze to bring you the *rognons de veau sautés vallée de Cousse* of your desire. After thawing them exquisitely, he may honor you by presenting them himself, saying, with quiet Gallic pride, *"Voila! M'sieu est servi!"*

Fundamental to the operation of an Old Stone Goose or of the pseudo-French restaurant is the restaurateur's presumption that his clientele has more money than brains; or that it has no taste; or that the clientele's level of taste is just as low as his; or that in any case the clientele will have so little knowledge of foodstuffs and of cuisine that it will be unable to distinguish prime from good and fresh from frozen, or know what the ingredients of Veal Parmigiana ought to be and how the dish should be cooked. It is possible, but difficult, to travel in France and Italy and eat badly in restaurants. Even the French have their Old Stone Geese in the form of quaint little inns full of copper pots, high prices, and cornstarch sauces. The rule, however, is that one eats well in European restaurants because the populace is extremely knowledgeable about food and cuisine, and expects and demands full value for the money it spends. Contrariwise, it is possible, but difficult, to dine out in America and eat well; Stone Geese represent the rule, not the exception. The reason for this is a national gastronomic innocence, combined with a middle-class assumption that the more anything costs, the better it must be.

I have said that choices other than Old Stone Geese are diminishing in the areas between drive-in fastfood snackstands and Geese, and between Geese and our handful of exquisite restaurants. Less than a lifetime ago it was possible to travel in America and find fresh, regional fare prepared in the kitchens of unpretentious restaurants. It was a time when names meant something. Many a small town restaurateur then raised the foods he cooked and served; more bought their supplies from local farmers. There were regional differences in America then, and the names on the menus meant something. You could find lobster in Maine, diamondback terrapin in Maryland, baked beans in Boston, and wild rice in Minnesota. Sweet potatoes and blueberries appeared on menus only in season. Today, these good American foods are increasingly absent from restaurants even in their native localities, although you may certainly find their names appearing on restaurant menus anywhere in America at any time of year. If your gastronomic memory is a long one, and if you order these foods today, you may be roundly disappointed if you will not also feel swindled.

Real lobsters are scarce even in Maine, where much of the catch sold on the piers comes in crates marked "imported from Nova Scotia." In Maine a lobster dinner can cost sixteen dollars. If a restaurant menu does not say "Maine lobster" and quote a price roughly equivalent to the French national debt, but says "lobster" or "lobster tail," you may be sure that you will be served not lobster, but the tail of a South American or South African crayfish.

Likewise, Maryland diamondback terrapin are scarce even in Maryland. Moreoever, their preparation for the stew pot is a messy, difficult process. If you see "terrapin soup" on the menu at any price lower than a lord's ransom, you may look forward to a green turtle, snapping turtle, or mock turtle soup.

By like token, the "Boston baked beans" on the menu will in all probability never have been baked in Boston, or even in the manner of Boston, but may have come from a can. There are several brands of canned baked beans on the market, all of them good in their own ways, but none of them has the unique flavor and texture of the genuine article. The "wild rice" you order may come from a box containing one grain of real wild rice to every 567,890 grains of brown rice or even hulled white rice. The sweet potatoes may come from a can, particularly if they are served candied, and the blueberries are far more likely to resemble hothouse blobs than berries gathered that day in the local berry patch.

The names on today's menus are therefore as disappointing or insulting as the distance between the genuine and the substitute. The many reasons for the substitutions include the scarcity of a food, the difficulty of its preparation, the high cost of labor, and the level of public taste. If a proprietor finds that his clientele cheerfully accepts his canned candied sweet potatoes, then he will just as cheerfully stop cooking and peeling fresh ones. If he finds people willing to pay near-lobster prices for crayfish, he will gladly sell crayfish at near-lobster prices. He will be guided by public taste, or the lack of it, and what is true of the

American restaurateur in this regard is true of many a European restaurateur as well. The more tourist-ridden the restaurant in London, Paris, or Rome, the more likely its dishes are to be approximations of, or substitutions for, genuine ones.

The public's taste, which is bound up with the public's reasons for dining in restaurants, and with its attitude toward food, its knowledge, and its expectations, has everything to do with any restaurant's existence. European families dine out much less frequently than American ones. They may, in fact, go to a restaurant only on rare and significant family occasions, such as weddings, confirmations, or particular anniversaries. Their selection of a restaurant will be based upon the establishment's reputation for the excellence of its food and wine; often for a restaurant's individual specialty. The family means to have a unique gastronomic experience as the focal point of a celebration. They expect and demand something extraordinary, a fact of which the restaurant's proprietor, waiters, and chef are all keenly aware. They will do their best not only out of pride and a desire to maintain their reputation, but also out of their desire to ensure the successful celebration of an important event.

American reasons for dining out are more general. One usual reason is to give everyone a change from Mom's home cooking, although we seldom put the thought quite that bleakly. We say, and also mean, we shall go out to give Mom a night out of the kitchen. In this case, we might order in a restaurant the same foods we would otherwise have at home: our desire is not for something special, but simply for a change of locale or for convenience. To the extent this is true, then it will be seen that the food we shall eat is not the reason why we have gone to the restaurant. Sometimes it is, as when we go to a Chinese restaurant to savor something exotic we ourselves do not know how to prepare. In that case, we cannot be the judges of the dishes we are served, because we do not know a thing in the world about them. Often enough, we go to a restaurant for the show it puts on, as in the case of the Wild West restaurant where the cowgirl waitresses fire blanks or the restaurant where the room spins to give the diner a revolving view of the city. Here, the food we are served is of secondary importance to the show. We also go to some restaurants because they are cheap and quick, as, for example, the drive-in fastfood snackstands are. The food in these places is actually expensive, when one considers what it is, but the drive-in is comparatively cheap when one considers the other possibilities. In any event, if money and speed are the primary reasons for patronizing a restaurant, then a concern for its food is a relatively minor matter.

In sum, we have many reasons other than a concern for food for going out to eat where we do and for going out as frequently as we do, and as a result we determine the quality, number, and kind of restaurants we have. In recent years, the American neighborhood restaurant, which used to serve unpretentious but generally acceptable homely fare at a reasonable price, has had a difficult time of it. The rising cost of labor, along with the rising cost of everything else, has been one of the difficulties. More important has been competition from the fastfood snackstand. "Let's face it," one restaurateur said. "People like hamburger. That's one thing. Then if they go to a drive-in, they don't have to dress decently. They can sit in the car in their undershirts.

"People aren't the same anymore," he said, "and neither are the neighborhoods. We used to have a nice neighborhood business for sixty years where we were, good food, nothing fancy, and then the neighborhood started to change and people left for the suburbs, and we had to move here. Where nobody knows us. All right, I said to my people, if they want hamburgers and french fries, we'll give them hamburgers and french fries; if they don't come to dinner but just want breakfast and lunch, we'll close the place at night and just serve coffee and Danish in the morning and hamburgers and french fries at lunch. It's either that or go out of business. What it is, is people, that's all it is."

Another restaurant, somewhat farther up the social ladder, found rising costs to be a controlling factor. To cut its costs, it began to buy frozen dinners from central suppliers, and even so it had to raise its prices. What used to be a restaurant that bought, prepared, and served its own foods for $3.85 became, in the space of five years, a restaurant selling airline food at $10.00. Here, the point to be made about airline food is not that the freezing process itself makes food *bad*. The texture, flavor, and nutritive value of a frozen food may be inferior to the fresh food, but not to the extent that the frozen food can be called bad. The trouble with airline food is rather that its manufacturer is not a *good cook*. If you find the taste of airline food difficult to recall, this is because a kind of corporate namby-pambyness was deliberately built into it. To give any mass-produced food product a strong taste or character is to run the risk of someone's not liking it. The idea is to produce a food that everyone will accept — which means a food that no one will like very much or will intensely dislike. The only problem this sort of food presented to the restaurant in question was that an ever decreasing number of customers were willing to pay $10.00 apiece for what they continued to think of as a $3.85 meal. Restaurants like this one, in the range between a drive-in and a Stone Goose, faced increasing difficulty as 1974 became 1975 and costs continued to rise so fast that prices printed on the menus had to be scratched out and new ones written in, and as patrons who had once appeared thrice a month now came but once a month, if at all.

Still surviving is a handful of exquisite American restaurants that cater to a discriminating clientele. One of these is situated in an elegant town house. No more than thirty patrons are served each evening; reservations are required. The dining rooms are small, each containing no more than four tables. The walls are covered not with paper, but with silk. The diners sit upon Chippendale chairs covered with needlepoint. The tables are set with damask, porcelain, crystal, and sterling, and with fresh-cut flowers in silver vases. The light is candlelight.

Here, the service is impeccable, constant, and unobtrusive. If this restaurant were in France, it would deserve Michelin's highest honors. The menu is brief: the proprietor himself selects the best of comestibles each morning at a specialty market. The menus given to the ladies have no prices on them. A simple dinner for two, consisting of a pâté, tournedos with sauce béarnaise and a garniture of vegetables, a salad, a bottle of Clos Vougeot '66, strawberries, coffee, and cognac, will cost more than sixty dollars. Patrons may pay by mail.

One of the couples at our table said they ate nowhere else when they dined out — but that they ate here only twice a year. The husband said that they had decided if they were going to spend money in restaurants, they might as well enjoy nectar and ambrosia in elegant surroundings twice a year, rather than spend the same money on twelve bad dinners in noisy clatter where waitresses ask "What's yours, Hon?"

He said he would also rather spend sixty dollars for one really wonderful meal than spend twenty dollars each for three mediocre ones in a Stone Goose, and that the trouble was there were no good restaurants in between the worst and the best. There used to be, he said, but not anymore. The middle range, he thought, had become a plethora of gimmicky deadfalls that serve bogus food at really high prices.

The great middlemass, reasonably affluent and relatively unlearned and uncaring about food, constitutes the proximate reason why the prices of everything are rising — much in the sense that a rich man's house, vacant for the summer and with its door ajar, constitutes an attractive nuisance to thieves. Of course merchants will charge all the traffic will bear; they have always done this and there is no necessary evil in the practice; they will continue to do it so long as there is traffic. You will recall that Senator Proxmire wonders if price-gouging in the supermarkets is not responsible for two thirds of the nation's inflation. But to speak of gouging is also to speak of the gouged. They must be able to pay the asked price; they must be willing to pay it; they are the ones to accept or reject among proffered wares. If they are naive, gullible, unlearned, and uncaring, possessed of money but not good taste, the merchants cannot be blamed for this. Nor can the merchants be expected to save the people from themselves, for this would be to suppose that merchants are a special order of altruistic, higher beings. In sum, if merchants gouge, it is with consent of the gouged. If our rent goes up, if our taxes increase, this is not entirely because of the landlord's greed or the expensive mistakes of politicians. It is partly because of what people are willing to pay for what they choose to buy. The causes of inflation are general: Whenever people have money, someone will take it away from them.

With respect to restaurants, we see what can be seen elsewhere. It is the middlemass that is responsible for the railroad sandwich and the airline dinner; the people who provide these things are, after all, only the caterers. When contracts are let to snackstand chains to operate the rest area eating facilities along a turnpike, it is the middlemass that both the turnpike authorities and the snackstand people have in mind. This middlemass is the primary reason for the existence of the convenience food industry, for the prevalence of drive-ins and Stone Geese. By reason of the inflationary force its buying habits exert, it is a principal reason why it is difficult for the neighborhood family restaurant to stay in business. Wherever Gresham's writ runs, the shoddy drives out the good.

That writ runs all the way along the food chain and throughout the restaurant business from the hamburger stand to the dining rooms of luxury hotels. Our ultramodern, expensive, and most widely advertised hotel chains are so many Stone Geese, linked together by toll-free 800 call numbers. In any one of them, breakfast is apt to consist of fake orange juice, a tiny serving of scrambled eggs made of dehydrated eggs, heat-and-serve frozen biscuits, and instant coffee (or tea in bags), for $4.70. All other meals in such hotels will likewise be airline food, served at stratospheric prices. A group of modern pilgrims recently sheltered in one of these inns; they were delegates to a national trade convention. Loud and bitterly did they lament the fare and the price thereof.

"The rooms are great, but my God, the food is terrible!" one of them said. "We paid twenty-five dollars last night for frozen dinners!"

Well should he know whereof he spake. Indeed, no one should know better, for he, like his fellows, represented a convenience food company. They were holding a trade fair of the products they sold to restaurateurs and hoteliers, and by evil chance the garbage they were served was their very own. They were Stoned, as it were, by one of their own Geese.

What's for Dinner Tonight?

Tales of Many Wives

If you are anything like me and most of my friends, you probably have a shelf full of cookbooks and a drawer full of recipes clipped from newspapers and magazines. And very likely, you use just one of the cookbooks regularly, and seldom open the drawer except to stuff another recipe into it. Usually, when you have friends in for dinner, you make a special effort, but only to the extent of serving them something you particularly like, have frequently yourself, and cook well. You never really cook up an adventurous storm in the kitchen except on quite special occasions. You are certainly interested in good food and good cooking, but generally speaking, you draw more vicarious pleasure from reading about food than actual pleasure from preparing it, although you do like to cook — but not every night.

More than likely, if you are like us, you haven't the faintest idea what you spent for food last week, although you have a very good idea what you spent at the supermarket. But some of the items in that shopping cart were not food, were they? There was soap, tissues, a packet of new dishcloths . . . And then, you did not figure in what was spent on lunch and coffee breaks at work, or what you spent at the restaurant last week, although that money was spent for food, too. If you did take these things into account and really know to the penny what you spent, you are unusual; most of us do not know, and, for that matter, most of us do not know as much about the food we buy as we think we know.

Such are among the general conclusions to be drawn from answers to a questionnaire I sent to eighty of our friends. Before we go an inch farther, I must make plain that the questionnaire was my own; that the respondents do not represent what a sociologist would call a valid random sample; that none of this is in any way scientific. The correlated results of the answers merely provide an interesting glimpse of the feeding habits, expenses, and attitudes of eighty households containing 227 people.

The eighty households include Jews, Protestants, and Catholics. Most of the respondents were women; most of them college-educated. Their residences range from a Vermont log cabin to a Park Avenue town house; their incomes, from $13,000 to $175,000 a year. The occupations of the householders include dressing hair, giving money to worthy causes, boarding up broken windows, teaching school, selling remnants at a department store, stockbroking, doing odd jobs, practicing law or medicine, and painting portraits. Our friends variously live in fifteen states and the District of Columbia, within a quadrilateral whose corners are Maine, Oregon, Texas, and Florida. The households consist of single young people, young married people without children, young married people with infants, middle-aged couples with teen-agers at home, unrelated people who live together, elderly retired couples, and single elderly people. The only things all these different people have in common are that they belong to the American middle class, they are friends of ours, and they were good enough to answer eighty-five questions about food — or so I supposed before I began to correlate their answers.

It then appeared that their attitudes and problems with respect to food, shopping, and cooking were remarkably similar, except that in the cases of single people the problems were less easy to solve because it is more difficult to buy for one person than it is to buy for several. For example, eggs are usually sold by the dozen, and many people do not eat a dozen eggs in a week. But apart from this, in no matter what section of the nation our friends lived, or in what sort of housing in city or country, and no matter what they do or earn, their expenses and eating habits fell into general patterns. If, in what follows, I seem to talk most of all about the middle-aged suburban housewife with children at home, this is merely reflective of the fact that such people made up the largest single group of respondents, and because, no matter how many people in the household might share in the buying and cooking, it was suburban Mom who most often drove to the shopping center and having brought home the bacon, cooked it.

The first similarity to be observed was that, with three exceptions, the respondents did nearly all of their shopping at a supermarket. Most of them bought their foodstuffs for an entire week in one trip, although some would go to the supermarket as often as three times a week. Distance from the store did not seem to be a factor, for whether the people lived in a city, its suburbs, exurbia, or open country, the general pattern was that they shopped once a week for food.*

---

* The three exceptions never went to supermarkets. Two of the households were vegetarian and patronized health food shops exclusively; in the third household the

What did they pay for it? That is difficult to say, because while most people knew what they had paid at the store, they did not always know how much of the money was spent on food and how much had been spent on something else. But most people had a general idea, and this worked out to an average of between thirty-eight dollars and fifty dollars for a household consisting of two middle-aged adults. This figure was consistent regardless of neighborhood, earnings, or geographical distribution. The fact that people we know spend similar amounts for their weekly food supply, no matter what state they live in, very strongly suggests that the nation's supermarkets follow a national pricing pattern. An exception was the Baltimore–Washington–Alexandria, Virginia, area, where the householders all spent between ten dollars and fifteen dollars more for food per week than the other respondents averaged. Four supermarket chains enjoy a shared monopoly in this area.

The answers next indicated that the size of the stomach, and how many stomachs there are in the household, and the ages of those stomachs have more to do with what our friends pay for food than any other factor. One not so wealthy family spent $150 a week at the store, but there were six children, between the ages of ten and twenty, at home. Here, the teen-age child may be described as a frenetically active, hungry, and thirsty bottomless pit. Worse, a teen-age child usually has friends who eat like vacuum cleaners. Many a mother sadly concluded, upon surveying a suddenly emptied larder, that the parents of her child's friends must starve their broods. Of course this is not the case: all teen-agers are locusts.

Taste and choice made no discernible difference in the respondents' food bills, nor did money in the bank. Those

---

maid telephoned orders to specialty shops, which made their deliveries to the servants' entrance.

whose favorite meal was spaghetti paid just as much for food per week as those whose favorite meal was roast beef, and so did the two vegetarian households. The wealthy spent the same amount for food as the not so wealthy spent — with the exception of the lady with the servants; her daily menu reads like that of a four-star Parisian restaurant. Otherwise, regardless of income, virtually all the respondents ate meat seven days a week, and many of them twenty-one times — some form of meat being served for breakfast, lunch, and dinner. Since what they all paid for their food was so remarkably similar, we must conclude that what they do *not* spend for meat must be spent on something else, so there is apparently a fixed cost to fill the American middle-class belly, no matter what you buy to fill it.

Interestingly, the overwhelming majority, including the wealthy, shop with a list, compare store prices, look for special sales, and pinch every penny they can — meanwhile complaining that food is costing them more this year than last, and saying they are worried about that. But why should the wealthy among them worry, when what they pay for food is a negligible proportion of their income? In answering one of the questions, the majority blamed the distributors, processors, and the federal government for rising food costs, rather than the farmers or the supermarkets. Thus their complaint was directed more at the society in which we live than at the quality of the food or at the store that sold it. However worried they might be about the rising cost of food, they were not buying any less of it. The general population might now be buying less food than it did a year ago, but not the middle class — if the people we know can be said to reflect the middle class.

When you go to the store, what do you buy? I'd be willing to bet that you buy beef, for instance, because beef is America's runaway favorite meat. But now, if you are anything like most of the people we know, I'd be tempted to bet that you do not know what all the cuts on a beef carcass are, and that you cannot tell aged beef from fresh beef by looking at it or even by tasting it.

I lose?

Very well; you are unusual. I shall have to win my money back from some other reader. Or maybe we can bet again about chicken. I'll bet you cannot tell the difference between a tender chicken and a tough one by looking at it. How about fish? How do you tell whether a fish is fresh? Can you tell whether an ear of corn is ripe without shucking it to peek?

In asking these questions, and others like them, I discovered that most of the people with whom I talked or to whom I wrote actually knew very little about what they were buying when they bought it — and I hasten to add that *I* didn't know as much about food as I thought I did until I became involved in the research for this book.

With respect to beef, almost all our friends were completely confused by the store names for the different cuts, only a few could say where the brisket was on the animal, and more than half had no idea what aged beef was or whether they should buy it. Less than one in four said they had some way of telling whether a chicken would be good to eat, and they said it should be blue, or pink, or dark yellow, or white, or that you should look at its feet.

"You can tell whether a fish is fresh by looking at its eyes," one woman said, "but I don't know after looking." A second woman said the only way she could tell was by seeing the fish swimming, while a third warned me, "If the top of the can bulges, don't buy it." Most of our friends said they trusted the man at the fish counter: if he said the fish was fresh, they would buy it. Similarly, a majority said they had no idea how to judge the ripeness of corn by superficial appearance, and their number included people who grew corn in their gardens.

If our ignorance about food is as general as I suspect it might be, this makes it all the easier for the producers, processors, and marketers to take advantage of us. It also suggests that while we all might want something good to eat for dinner tonight, we will be lucky if we get it. Of course it is also possible that while we all might be naive about foodstuffs in general, we may indeed be well informed about those that we customarily select — but this in turn would suggest that we are less venturesome in the kitchen than we might wish we were. The remedy for all this, if we are to have a serious interest in what we are going to have for dinner tonight, is to become knowledgeable about appearance and quality. Any cooking course worthy of the name begins with teaching the students how to judge the quality of what they see in the markets.

Let us say you have now come out of the supermarket with a week's supply of food in brown paper bags. Now, without looking into those bags, how much do you think you spent for frozen foods? What percentage of your food money went for snacks, and for convenience foods, such as TV dinners or packaged dinners like prepared macaroni and cheese?

Our friends' answers to these questions formed another interesting pattern. If you guess that you spend no more than 5 percent of your weekly food money on frozen foods, you exactly agree with the majority of my respondents. If you say you never buy snacks except when company is coming, or that you spend less than 5 percent of your money for snacks and then just to have them in the house in case someone drops in, you would agree with six out of every eight people we know. And if you said you *NEVER!* buy TV dinners or other convenience foods, with the capitals, the italics, and the exclamation point being your way of saying this, then you see eye to eye with seven out of every eight people we know. One gathers that if the convenience food industry exists at all, it does so without the support of the middle class.

Well . . . maybe. And maybe not.

Let us look at all this again, for there is another pattern to consider. Nearly all of our respondents said they served frozen orange juice for every breakfast, and the majority added that they served frozen vegetables three times a week, if not more often — but that they spent only 5 percent of their weekly food money for frozen foods. Let us suppose they spend $50.00 a week for food, and that the household consists of two adults. Five percent of $50.00 is $2.50, and I doubt that anyone can serve two glasses of orange juice every day and frozen vegetables three or more times a week at a total cost of $2.50.

A similar discrepancy appears with respect to snacks. *None* of the respondents reported spending more than 10 percent on snacks, and the crowded majority said 5 percent or less. But when asked how they might reduce their food costs by 20 percent, more than one in every four said they would stop buying snacks and others said they would cut out frozen foods! This leads me to suspect that when people say they *NEVER!* buy convenience foods they mean to say, "Well, hardly ever."

I think the answers suggest something other than an inability to do arithmetic. I think the pattern is that we all believe we should not spend as much as we do for frozen foods and, feeling somewhat guilty for not having bought fresh ones, we tend to minimize what we actually spent. Or, perhaps, when someone comes up and asks us, we subconsciously tend to put ourselves in a better light by implying we are more independent of the frozen food industry than we really are. This strikes me as being even more true with respect to snacks and convenience foods. Since the public air is full of derision for the junk food, bellywash, and TV dinner industries, it is fashionable to say we never have that stuff in the house — except of course to feed our friends who come to call! — and we *NEVER!* eat convenience dinners (which would imply laziness or worse).

To linger on the matter for one moment more: when asked how they could reduce their weekly food bill by 20 percent, only three of our eighty respondents came up with an answer that impressed my wife and me as being the probably correct one. We wish we had thought of it ourselves. One of our friends put it thus:

> This is a long story I had better put my mind to. The easy answer is to cut out meat. One or two meatless days would cut the bill — but not by 20%. There are no cheap cuts of meat. Even canned corned beef costs money. So the cut *will have to be across the board* — smaller servings of meat (one quarter pound per person is adequate); check the vegetables. Getting a can for 45¢ instead of 50¢ saves 10%. Cut way down on luxury items like cauliflower and asparagus (sigh). I find budget recipe books a dreadful fraud — they take ½ pound of lion meat — the kind they throw to lions at the Zoo — and cover it with mushrooms and cheeses, all of which adds a ridiculous amount to the cost. Rather a small piece of sirloin which sometimes costs even less than chuck. Anyway, you can't cut one thing, you have to cut right across the board.

All of our respondents shared the current national concern for proper nutrition, as I presume you do, too. But do you know what the ingredients of a proper diet are? Only one in ten of our friends listed all the necessary ingredients of such a diet. Only three in every eight read the list of ingredients on cans and packages as often as "sometimes," and, despite all the recent publicity about RDA labels, seven out of every eight of our friends either never looked at them or had never heard of them. Yet their answers to other questions indicated that everyone was receiving what was needed, if not more than was needed, to keep body and soul together. For example, although almost everyone failed to list leafy greens, or roughage, as a necessary part of the diet, everyone ate salads several times a week if not every day in the week, and their purchases otherwise included reasonable amounts of all that was necessary. Whether their selections were based on family custom, intuition, or upon a classroom education that could not be remembered in precise detail, or even upon taste, is quite impossible to say. What can be said, however, is that most shopped in supermarkets and returned home with foodstuffs that would properly nourish them. The point to be made here about supermarkets is that, while much of the food on their shelves is junk and much else is of poor quality and of limited variety, it is quite possible to buy the ingredients of a proper diet in a supermarket. As, indeed, almost everyone that we questioned does. Yet half of our friends thought that their diet was now worse than it was three years ago, and blamed the food processors for this. In response to another question, half of them refused to believe that America was the best-fed nation on earth, maintaining that although we do have plenty to eat too much of it is junk. What I gather from this is that at least half of the people we know are suspicious of our food supply system, believing that the nutritional quality of its products is worsening and that people other than themselves are buying trash foods — and that this situation should not exist. Whether this is in fact the case is neither here nor there with respect to the immediate question. What is important is that everyone is concerned, half of them suspiciously so, and I would say that such a concern is a hopeful one.

Equally pregnant with change were the answers to questions relevant to cooking. There used to be an expression "as American as apple pie," by which we all meant "Mom's apple pie." But I suspect the truth of the matter is that Mom never baked an apple pie, although Granny might very well have done so, and that your mother did not teach you to cook apple pie or anything else. If you are like most of the people we questioned, you taught yourself to cook, you do very little baking except at Christmas time or birthdays, and when you bake, you most likely never bake pie. I presume the decline of the tradition — that mother taught daughter — began when the voice of Fanny Farmer was heard in the land and the deluge of cookbooks began. Most of our friends say they have more than ten cookbooks; thirty is a quite usual number; one woman we know has a hundred. Most of us watch Julia Child on television; more than half the people we know clip the food columns regularly; and not a few have traveled abroad and their foreign experience has affected their cookery. The overall picture, as constructed from what our friends report, is that of self-taught cooks preparing a more adventurous cuisine than the one they had known as children. Roast beef is the favorite meal by a wide margin, but after this, in order of preference, come lasagna, spaghetti, chicken, steak, fish, roast lamb, lamb chops, beef stew, Mexican food, vegetable or meat casseroles, vegetarian meals, pork chops, beef stroganoff, veal, spare ribs, sausage and lentils, oxtail stew, and Japanese food. The chicken, fish, and other meats are often prepared by European methods. Most of our friends were aware of specialties in their regions, as, for example, the New Englanders were aware of the baked bean, but in no case was the regional specialty anyone's favorite food — with the exception of seafood in the coastal areas. Such eclecticism invites speculation. One inference is that there exists a bored lack of interest; that one thing is as acceptable as any other. The opposite inference is that there is a desire for experiment and change for the better.

Our friends' answers support both inferences. Our cookery would seem rather like the bottle that the pessimist observes to be half empty and that the optimist sees to be half full. To take the worse first, we find almost exactly half of our friends reporting that they either like to cook only once in a while, or that they hate the kitchen and everything about it, or that they do not give a damn for cooking one way or another — it is just something you have to do every day whether you like it or not. Patterns of work have nothing to do with this. Those of our friends who are employed outside the home spend exactly as much time shopping and preparing the dinners as do those who have no outside jobs — and they enjoy this just as much or just as little. It would next appear, if these eighty middle-class households should be representative of any other than themselves, that the table occupies no high place in the American system of priorities. For example, one in every four families eats dinner while watching television, which at the very least suggests their entire attention is not devoted to their food. No one dresses formally for dinner. Once, when there were still Englishmen in jungles, a good many of the middle class did — but that seems long ago and in another country. Today it would seem that more than half of us come to table as we are, to eat in the kitchen or television room, and there bolt down whatever it is in less than half an hour. So it would appear that on a day-to-day basis, our interest in food is that of food-as-food, rather than in food as a kind of religious mystery to be celebrated according to a ritual in a special sanctuary adorned with the gifts of art.

The other view, that the bottle is half full, is supported by the almost exactly half of our friends who say they either like to cook or love to do so, and do not qualify this by saying "sometimes." I am well aware that some people will refuse to believe that anyone really likes to cook, much less loves to do so all the time, and all I can say to the doubtful is that I have reason to believe otherwise. Further, those who like to cook are uniformly adventurous in their cuisine. It would also seem that, if there is not always the aspect of a celebration at every dinner time, the idea of a dinner as a celebration is by no means dead. Virtually all of the eighty families look forward to large family holiday feasts, even if not everyone enjoys preparing them and cleaning up afterward. On these occasions, something is added to food other than considerations of taste, cost, and nourishment. So it also appears when most of the eighty families entertain their friends: something special is prepared; the dinner is served in the dining room; the table has been set with particular care.

And so it also is when the family goes out to eat: the expectation is of something special, served in a special ambiance. Money is scarcely an object, nor is food-as-food of any matter, for very few respondents said they could eat in a "good" restaurant for less than $20.00 a couple, which is either almost two thirds or almost one half of what they say they spend for an entire week's supply of food. You will recall that the eighty households are scattered across America. It is at least interesting to learn that more than five in every eight of these people expect to spend between $20.00 and $60.00 for dinner for two, with the largest number of them expecting the cost to be up to $30.00. You may pessimistically presume that the cost of eating out in America is outrageous, or you may optimistically presume that the people who pay such a price are willing to pay it for something they believe to be good. Would you, for example, go to a restaurant if the bill for two was $60.91, and would you go there if someone else paid the bill? When asked this double question, one in eight said of course they'd go, and more than half said they'd certainly go if someone else were paying. Only three in eight said no to both parts of the question, giving as their reason that this was simply too much to pay for food. Evidently, the majority believed that a good restaurant served something more than food, and I regard this, too, as a hopeful sign.

The same reason to hope was suggested in quite another way, when only two of the eighty families said they frequently see the inside of a McDonald's hamburger stand, a Howard Johnson, a Colonel Sanders, or any other fastfood snackstand, unless they find themselves trapped on a highway while traveling, with no alternative in sight. If our respondents should be representative of their peers, then it would seem that the national chains of snackstands, like TV dinners, simply do not exist insofar as the middle class is concerned. Unfortunately, the huge majority of those who replied *NEVER!* to the question did not go on to give their reasons. Perhaps they meant to say they thought the food was atrocious or that it cost too much for what it was, either of which seems a reasonable argument to me. Or perhaps their objection was not only to the food, but also to the redundant and mechanical aspects of a kind of massfood-for-massman swilling station, in which you are trapped in an ambiance that makes a travesty of dining. That, too, would seem a reasonable argument to me, particularly in light of the respondents' answers to other questions.

Taken all in all, and when compared with other reports of what is going on in the land, the answers of the eighty families encourage me to believe that we may be standing on the threshold of a gastronomic renaissance, or at least upon a rung of a ladder leading to it. We might not know what food costs, but we are finding that out; we might not know what food should look like, but we are finding that out, too. We are also no longer taking for granted that whatever we are offered at the store has nutritional value, and we are learning that food is more than simply fuel. The step beyond that is learning how good food can be when prepared in other than cursory ways, and that step is being taken. Most of us seem to be aware of the possible pleasures of the table, and are aware, too, that good cookery is not the only source of those pleasures; amateur theatrics are also a part of a pleasurable dinner: the scene must be set, and the actors have their roles.

The last step, from the elevation of a concern for dining to the status of a generally shared form of art, would bring us to the threshold of an American gastronomic renaissance. Whether we take such a step will, however, depend on our willingness to make substantial changes in our way of life, and I am happy to be able to report that the next chapters will show that some of us are beginning to take that step.

How to Survive
in the
Land of More

America: Take It or Leave It

The way we live nowadays determines what we eat, and this situation is very new. We have seen that Grandpa ate exceedingly well, feasting on a great variety of good things, but that he had to pay for this by working hard from dawn to dusk, bound to his land. In his day, what he ate determined the way he lived. Nowadays, most of us live easily in cities, bound to nothing except our simple jobs, but we have to pay for this by being fed a diminished variety of second-rate foods, supplied to us by a system we did not intentionally devise, but into which we rather quickly slipped, and into which, like quicksand, we more and more rapidly sank.

The question is what to do about it. It would seem to follow that if we cannot stand the food around here, we had better move out or otherwise make some changes in the way we live. We could doubtless eat better if most of us moved back to the land, but it is idle to pretend that most of us could do this or would want to. Moreover, this would imply moving America back to Square One, and that is too much to expect. In any case, few of us have such an option. Compounding the problem is the apparent fact that most Americans do not object to the American way of life and the food that goes with it, for otherwise we would never have tolerated, much less created, our urban sprawl, corporate farms, processed foods, supermarket networks, and nation-wide chains of cheapjack fastfood snackstands. The number of the acquiescent forms such a tremendous majority as to diminish choice and to make dissent difficult. The minority of the dissatisfied is not so small as to be insignificant or to be without effect, but it seems to me that those who wish to escape from the disappointing aspects of American life will have to do so upon an individual basis. In all that follows, I cannot be prescriptive, nor would I want to be if I could, but I can and will report upon what some people are doing in the way of creating differences that are valuable to themselves. All their efforts involve taking time from one thing in order to devote it to another. Thus it would appear that the quality of life is directly related to the choices we make in how we spend the time of our lives. A family named O'Hara has been thinking along just these lines, and they can serve as a first and modest example:

Like most American families today, the O'Haras consist of the basic unit of husband, wife, and children. No other relatives live in the household or even in the same city. Once all four children were in school, each member of the family became busy with affairs that were different from those of every other member, and none of them saw or thought of one another all day long.

They do not eat breakfast together, because Frank leaves

for his job at one time, Mary for hers at another, and the children for school at a third. Whatever the breakfast, it is something easily and quickly prepared and consumed, a standard meal served day after day, year in and year out, without the slightest variation. It is, in a way, an unnoticed meal, a thing of habit, like putting on your shoes. Who is conscious of tying his shoes? No more are the O'Haras conscious of breakfast. Sundays are exceptions, however. The simple orange juice, toast, and coffee are then elaborated upon to include pancakes or waffles with bacon or sausage. Lunch is nonexistent as a family meal. The parents eat at their jobs; the children, at school. Dinner provides the only occasion on which all members of the family are together. However commonplace this kind of family life might be in modern America, it impressed Frank and Mary as being both unnatural and unsatisfactory, and they are doing what they can to arrange things differently.

"Mary and I are in the midst of constructing our own version of the 'modern marriage,'" Frank wrote to me.

> Neither of us subscribes to the "women's place is in the home" attitude. Of course, I hasten to add that the man's place is not in the home, either, not by a long shot. So, our attitude toward food, the preparation, consuming and disposal of it, has evolved into a family affair. After ten years of my working and going to school, and with Mary staying home with the kids, and the consequent eat-and-run approach, we are now determined to share the gustatory duties by spreading them among the whole family. This is not merely a necessity due to the fact that we both work, but a positive attitude shared by all of us, that the mealtime should be a family get-together time, just like the old days. And besides, we love to eat.

His letter went on to say that each member of the family cooks the evening meal one night each week, with everybody pitching in on Saturday. The Sunday dinner, a four-course feast accompanied by wine, is the looked-forward-to best meal of the week, and this is prepared by Mary. Each Sunday dinner is different from the last.

"Inflation being what it is," Frank wrote, "each member of the family is encouraged to try some new creative way of serving hamburger (except, of course, as served with a peanut butter sauce, which Sean once suggested to no avail.)" Sean, the youngest, would put peanut butter on everything if he had his way. "We have gone to cookbooks, to our own peasant intuition, to do imaginative things with hamburger," the letter said, "and sometimes we manage to make it taste like hamburger."

Those who do not cook the meal take turns in setting the table and cleaning up afterward. Everyone is encouraged to bake whatever he wishes any time he pleases. Efforts are made to balance the diet.

"With regularity, I buy turnips, rutabagas, eggplant, collard greens, and cook them up — and no one eats them," Frank wrote.

Truthfully, these attempts at introducing vitamins into the diet in the form of less attractive vegetables are not an unqualified success. But I do feel that everyone should try these things — they are not forced to eat more than a taste of them. Fresh fruit, soy beans, sunflower seeds and dried apricots are always around for snacks. We see nothing wrong with having a snack between meals, as long as it is a real food that is good for you, and not some junk food that is bad for you. Besides, real food costs less than junk food in terms of money and nutrition. About once every three weeks I start a huge pot of soup, dump in all fresh vegetables and a soup bone and let the mess cook in its own juice. We eat this with hard bread and cheese until it is gone. Each meal has a salad — and at least one vegetable, and meat or fish.

In truth, all these efforts are attempts to fight against the prevailing influence of McDonald's and Arthur Treacher's Fish & Chips. We must fight the temptation, because of our schedule, to settle for a "99-center," or its equivalent. In all, we are successful most of the time in making the meals an enjoyable time, by having each member of the family become in turn the chef whose creative efforts we praise and look forward to. We are a family trying to prepare both the boys and the girls to enjoy the preparation of food as a hobby, not as an obsession.

They are also a family fighting against the divisiveness and loneliness that characterize urban American life, trying to create something of a family life during the one daily opportunity they have to meet together and offer something of themselves to one another. They are not simply eating food or experimenting in the culinary arts; they are holding daily communion together in the land of the Philistines. They are also finding this difficult to do, because of the pressures put upon them by their different work schedules, which often require one or another of them to stay late at work.

"Right now," Frank wrote, "I'd say we cook and serve fresh, personally prepared meals seventy percent of the time. The rest of the time, we buy and consume all manner of store-bought, frozen, packaged, or otherwise distilled food. But Mary and I are determined that the children will respect good food, know how to buy it and prepare it, and above all, form good taste in the enjoyment of meals as a gathering place for family and friends."

I believe the thought and care a family gives its dinner table is directly related to that family's view of itself. It is my experience that the best tables are set by the happiest and most closely knit families, and that the quality of the food is only one of the factors that makes the meal a success. The other factors have to do with the atmosphere within which the meal is served — and the atmosphere will certainly express the feelings the family members have for one another and for their guests. Ordinarily, I would prefer to eat almost anything other than spare ribs, but I have feasted on spare ribs in the company of a loving family.

For example, the Agnello family brings a quality of fiesta to all of its evening meals, even though the food itself might be nothing more than sausage, scrambled eggs, toast, and salad. The special quality owes not a little to the care with which the table is set. The family is by no means a wealthy one, but it does not reserve what sterling, crystal, and porcelain it has for special occasions. Instead, the Agnellos use their best tableware every day, arguing that there is no point in having good things unless you use them. They light their table with candles, even though the candles they burn sometimes cost more than the main course — as is true whenever they prepare a dish of lamb kidneys or chicken livers. Like many another family these days, all members of the family share in the cooking and in the kitchen chores, because all of them agree there is neither point nor justice in saddling just one person with all the work, and they are fond of saying that, since they must all live in the same house, everyone must pull his oar. If someone in the family cooks the meal, someone else cleans up afterward. But the usual pattern is that everyone contributes both to the cookery and to the kitchen police.

This family does not frequently entertain, but when it does, the quality of fiesta takes on an additional dimension, even if the food does not. When the two children, a boy and a girl, were still in grammar school, they began to act as butler and maid — for which they received a fee. The boy solemnly takes the guests' wraps in the hallway and announces the guests to his parents in the living room. There are never more than two other couples because, the father explained, when there are more than six at table, the host and hostess cannot do full justice to each of their friends.

They make place cards for the table and corsages for the ladies. Attention is paid to the color of the flowers in terms of the colors the ladies customarily favor. The foodstuffs are chosen not only with respect to their complementary flavors, but also with respect to their colors as well. At the ladies' places, in addition to the small corsages, there are small hand-printed menus that describes the courses and bear the date of the occasion.

When everyone is seated within this carefully set scene, the young butler pulls the cork (or more often unscrews the cap) and, with a white towel over his arm, first pours a drop or so in his father's glass for approval. The young maid serves the antipasto while the butler pours the wine.

The youngsters serve to the forks and clear from the spoons, remember never to engage in personal conversation with the guests no matter if the guests invite this, and otherwise act as servants, in order, the father explained, to be able to command when they should be grown and have households of their own. In between the courses, the children do the dishes in the kitchen, because the family has so few dishes that those used for the antipasto have to be pressed into service again for the apples.

In sum, a feeling of mannered elegance is created, all of which helps to raise the cheap wine to a level it does not always deserve, and to imply that the *spaghetti alla carbonara* consists of something more splendid than pasta, eggs, pepper, fat bacon, and cheese. It helps, too, to explain what the Agnellos think of themselves and their friends.

Upon hearing of the Agnellos, a mother named Joan Marlowe said, "May I remind you that today's young are not the first to share cooking and household chores? There are just more of them doing this now. Many women have had understanding husbands who helped. This isn't just *some* women's thing. My husband and our sons have helped me for years, and especially with preparing for parties."

All members of the Marlowe family are employed, and they have a practical reason for cooperation. Time is in short supply in the Marlowe household, which is a family of commuters. There are fewer people in the American household today than there were in Granny's time, and for most of the day there may be none at all, as is the case with the Marlowes. While we have a plethora of modern machines to help speed the household chores, the basic amount of work has remained the same, and although we now have an eight-hour work day, the working day has not been shortened for those who, like the Marlowes, must spend three hours of every working day in their lives going back and forth in glass and metal capsules between country home and city job.

Yet it seems to me that the real reason for family cooperation in the kitchen goes past practicality to embrace understanding. Apparently, what is becoming more widely understood is the family's need to establish itself as a family. I think this is the common thread that ties the O'Hara, Agnello, and Marlowe families together with many another. In this context, I suggest we reread Frank O'Hara's letter between the lines.

He begins by saying that neither he nor his wife believes the woman's place is in the home. He adds that the man's place is not in the home by a long shot. This reflects a prevalent American belief that the home is restrictive and the work done in it is a form of mindless slavery, whereas work done outside the home is exciting, broadening, and fulfilling.

I cannot think of another nation on earth that takes so

light a view of the home, or that so generally reduces the family to the basic unit of Mom, Pop, and the kids — and then separates them every day. Everyone else in the world seems to realize that the family comes first, even if the work done outside the home should actually prove to be exciting and fulfilling — instead of being what it usually is, which is boring and cretinizing. Everyone else also seems to know that the family unit should not be narrowed to man, woman, and child.

Much as we Americans might yield to the modern notion, I think we know or feel that it is wrong. Thus we find Frank O'Hara waxing nostalgic for "a family get-together time, just like the old days." Thus, I think, we might explain the growing popularity of communal living among the young: it could be construed as a search for a surrogate for the extended family. In any case, before the proliferation of our technological society, the woman's place was in the home, and so was everyone else's. There is no place like home. There never was any place like it. The O'Haras sense this, and so do the Agnellos and the Marlowes and so I think do all others who seek to make whatever home they can in whatever time they have for this. As families have always done, they first fasten their attention upon the food that keeps them all alive. Then, by virtue of how they prepare and eat their food, they seek to establish a family identity in a society that otherwise regards them as so many slightly different Social Security numbers.

"In truth," we find Frank O'Hara concluding, "all these efforts are attempts to fight against the prevailing influence of McDonald's . . ."

I daresay he is using the name of a national chain of swilling stations in a symbolic sense as well as in a literal one: he is telling us we need to find ways of making the American rat race somewhat less ratty. He ends by saying that the pressures on his family are so great that its efforts are only 70 percent successful.

He is at least in better case than the complainers, who moan that the work they do leaves them no time but to open cans or to take something — anything — out of the refrigerator and call it dinner. The complainers say they do not like to do this, and I do not believe a word of it. I believe that everyone does what he *really* wants to do. If food were really important to the complainers, there are many opportunities open to them. For example, they could always stop buying the cans, packages, and frozen dinners they say they do not like. The difference between preparing a dinner from fresh foods and a dinner of convenience foods is, after all, a matter of minutes, not hours. Who cannot find the minutes?

Then, if it should appear that the minutes cannot be found and that patterns of work are actually determining what the people eat and how and where and when they eat it — *and if the complainers actually find this situation intolerable* — such people can always do what others have done. They can move closer to where they work. They can look for some other line of work that would give them more time to be themselves — if they *really* believed their lives were more important to them than the work they did. I know families who have made exactly these choices. They were not, however, complainers.

A working mother in Washington, D.C., as pressed for time as anyone could be, creates more time in her day by the simple expedient of rising at six and using the early morning to prepare all the ingredients she will cook at dinner time. If you wonder *who wants to rise at six,* the answer is that this woman does. She is a splendid and imaginative cook. She enjoys setting a good table. Food is important to her. So is her household and so is her family. She would rather get the preparations for supper out of the way in the morning, and get much of her housework done, than start picking up the house and beginning the meal from scratch at the end of her eight-to-five day, when her children and husband return from their schools and office to command a share of her attention. She says she likes the quiet of the early morning hours, when she has time alone to create something valuable to share with others.

Complainers will never be escapers. What all escapers have in common is sufficient power of will to be able to turn off the television set and otherwise close their eyes, ears, and minds to whatever it is that everyone else is supposed to be buying and doing, in order that they can identify their own needs. Finally, they have sufficient imagination to grasp this sorry scene entire, and mold it closer to heart's desire. It is not always difficult to do this.

For example, it does no good to complain that there are nothing but fastfood snackstands along our turnpikes and superhighways. It is perfectly possible to drive all day and enjoy a delicious luncheon en route. You can leave Philadelphia at eight in the morning, average fifty miles an hour along the Pennsylvania Turnpike, stop an hour for lunch, and then press on, arriving in Pittsburgh at four in the afternoon. At almost exactly the halfway point there is a town called Breezewood. There are no woods and little breeze, and it is not really a town, but a collection of motels, billboards, neon signs, filling stations, and snackstands. This is where the buses, plying between the two cities, break their trips. You can acquire a turkey sandwich and a cup of coffee in Breezewood for $4.40, not including tax and tip. The turkey sandwich is served on a platter, the size of a small basin, that is brimming with a kind of yellow custard. Beneath this, you will find a slice or two sawed from a turkey that had been drowned in its old age. Under these bits, there will be a soggy paste that had once been two slices of store bread. The sandwich will be as preposterously inedible as the weak coffee is undrinkable. This may be attributed to any of the following:

First, motorists and bus passengers are willing to pay, or feel they must pay, $4.40 for inedible swill and undrinkable bellywash.

Second, most of the people who travel America's highways believe that such food is good and that the price is fair.

Third, the proprietor of the snackstand does not understand food, or likes what he prepares, or has a contempt for mankind, or all three.

In fairness to Breezewood, I must say that what happens there is no worse than what happens in other roadside snackstands from one ocean to the other. It is also possible to eat wonderfully well in Breezewood, as two young Greyhound bus passengers did.

They dined comparatively cheaply on delicious cold shrimp dipped into an excellent homemade mayonnaise, upon equally delectable sandwiches made of chicken breasts, homebaked bread, and lettuce. They followed this with fresh fruit and cheese, and enjoyed, meanwhile, a good cold white wine. When they opened the basket they had thoughtfully brought along with them and began to dip the shrimps into the mayonnaise, a passenger sitting across from them wondered if the young people would not like to read her newspaper. When they politely declined, the woman sighed and joined the rest of the passengers, who were now leaving the bus to lunch upon the $4.40 turkey sandwich.

The young people, who turned out to be newlyweds, were intelligent escapers from one of the more flatulent aspects of American life. They had discovered that the thing to do when traveling was to take a picnic along; that this was invariably bound to be less expensive and better than whatever was offered along the road; that one could escape from the overpriced garbage of the snackstand by the simple expedient of fetching along something that was actually good to eat.

Similarly, office workers are condemned to the company cafeteria or neighborhood luncheonette only if they wish to be. At least one group of workers has made a successful escape. Each worker brings for lunch something he or she has bought or prepared or wishes to cook on the office hotplate the group purchased. When lunch hour arrives, all of them push desks together to form a kind of refectory table, and enjoy a cooperative repast that customarily includes fruit and wine, and that otherwise consists of favorite foods each wishes to share with others. "Since all of us like to cook and eat," one of them said, "our lunches are something special."

All sorts of escapes are possible to those who possess the willingness to take the time and make the effort to break out of America's gastronomic jail. It is even possible to enter a supermarket and escape with something that will be good for you to eat, and that you can obtain without having to enter into involuntary bankruptcy. The number of successful escapers from the supermarket's high prices is much larger than any supermarket manager wishes it were.

"It's so simple," one woman said. "Just buy fresh foods. They have fresh foods in the supermarket, too, along with all that processed slop. Shop with a list and buy only what is on the list."

She was one of those indomitable mothers who are strong enough to listen, unmoved, to a child wailing for whatever new taste thrill is being advertised on television and devoured by every other little videot in the neighborhood. Like other children, hers too sing the food jingles they hear on television; unlike the others, her children never get such food — at least, not at home.

It is often possible to escape from supermarkets entirely.

In cities where farmers' markets exist, people will shop in those markets. Others will join food cooperatives. Escapers will, when they can, buy picking rights in fields. To whatever extent they can, they will grow their own food.

I believe that something other than a desire to save money characterizes all such activities. In the case of such farmers' markets as those in Portland, Oregon, and Boston, Massachusetts, and many another city in between, people will travel a considerable distance to enjoy the feeling such a market gives them. The notion that prices are low is often a rationalization, because *all* the foodstuffs in farmers' markets are not *always* better than or even as good as their supermarket equivalents, nor are they *always* cheaper. But there is always a feeling, born of sight, scent, and sound, that there never is in a supermarket — and a sense of rich profusion. There is a feeling that when one deals with a man at a stall bright with fresh produce, one is dealing directly with someone who, if not the farmer himself, is at least close to the soil or in any case stands behind his produce both literally and figuratively. For reasons that are not always justifiable, the customers feel more confident in the open-air market than they feel in the supermarket. If the market should be an exotic one, as it is in Philadelphia, there is the additional feeling of adventure in a foreign land. In sum, the customer's escape from the supermarket is an escape from more things than unconscionable markups.

By like token, joining a food cooperative is something more than an escape from high prices. It is an adventure undertaken with others in search of an alternative. By my definition, a food cooperative is any group of people who band together to procure food.

In a simple form, a cooperative could be a group of neighbors who pile into an automobile belonging to one of them and drive off to the nearest farm to buy picking rights.

The term means that, for a small sum paid the farmer, they have the right to go into his fields and pick, let us say, a peck of peppers. The sum may be slightly more or less than what the farmer would receive from a huckster or a commission merchant, but it will always be far lower than any market price. Having filled the car trunk with produce, the neighbors drive back to town and divide the load. To be sure, they will have saved something in the cost of gasoline by using one car rather than several and they will have bought food cheaply, but equally important, if not more so, they will have had a pleasant day in the country and the even more pleasant feeling of having done something for themselves.

A variation of this kind of cooperation is for the neighbors to rent a truck, which a volunteer drives to farms or wholesale outlets, or to supermarkets when an actual bargain is advertised as a loss leader. Even after the truck rental is paid, the food is had cheaply. But once again more is involved than a consideration of cost. Neighboring counts for something too — particularly when in urban America there is so little opportunity for people to offer something of value to one another.

A food cooperative in Vermont takes the form of a group of townsfolk who rent a patch of ground in common, divide among themselves the costs and chores of gardening it, and divide the harvest according to what they mutually agree to have been the value of each person's contribution. This last bit is always rather tricky and demands everyone's forbearance.

On a more complicated level, the members of a food cooperative may rent a truck to acquire foodstuffs from farmers and/or wholesalers, and then prepare these foodstuffs for freezing in a commonly owned or rented food locker. The total cost of such an operation is once again lower than the collective price all the people would have paid if each had bought the same amount of frozen food in a supermarket.

In an even more complicated form, a food cooperative may consist of hundreds of people who buy shares of stock and have equal voting rights, no matter how many shares they own, in a corporation that does a profitable business. The corporation buys food from farmers and/or wholesalers and sells it from its own retail store. The store has a paid manager and staff, and the prices will closely match those in the local supermarkets. The store is open to the public as well as to the members of the cooperative. No one saves money at the time of purchase by shopping in this store. The members of the cooperative will, however, retain their checkout counter receipts. At the end of its fiscal period, the cooperative will share its profits among the members, each of whom receives a share that takes into account the *sum of his purchases* at the store — as evidenced by the receipts he now presents. Thus the members buy their food at cost. In effect, the members of such a cooperative escape shopping in a supermarket by operating a supermarket of their own, and in such a system it is theoretically (if not actually) possible for the members to receive free food and money into the bargain.

The kind and number of food cooperatives are limited only by the imagination and willingness to work together that exist among any particular group of people, and what they all have in common is the members' desire to break free from a system that holds the nation in thrall. I think much the same thing can be said of gardening.

In 1974, the urge to keep a garden was so widespread as to cause seed companies to report record sales, and to bring about a sudden and unexpected shortage of home canning equipment in the nation's hardware stores. The *New York Times* was as surprised as anyone else by this unlooked-for phenomenon.

"Not since World War II Victory Gardens," the *Times* said, "have so many inflation-harried weekend farmers scratched around in their backyards, the vacant lot, or even the Manhattan patio, trying to coax up home-grown fruits and vegetables to supplement store-bought staples."

Let the *Times* think what it will, I shall remain convinced that the rising food prices that year were at most catalytic or mnemonic agents, and that the nationwide enthusiasm for gardening had nothing to do with money and only a little more to do with food. I have yet to meet or hear of anyone, except for professional truck gardeners, to whom money is either the principal or exclusive reason for their agricultural activity. Indeed, the examples cited in the body of the *Times*'s article refuted the thesis stated in its first paragraph. One of them described a New York editor who set out a garden in the patio of his fashionable brownstone, and said he spent so much for the earth that he bought by the bag, that he hated to leave it outdoors at night. Obviously, money was no object to him, and then, as it turned out, neither was the food. He said he just liked "to see their mouths drop open" when he told his suburban colleagues that he was growing seven-feet-high tomato plants, along with eggplants, string beans, celery, basil, green peppers, lettuce, and cucumbers in midtown Manhattan — with no interference from groundhogs or moles.

If the New York editor was gardening as a kind of party trick, others also were finding their way back to the land for reasons of enjoyment. An accountant turned to gardening as a kind of busman's holiday. He first worked out on paper the start-up cost of a vegetable garden, worked out a schedule of possible annual yields, studied the selling-price curve of produce in the supermarkets, made an extrapolation, and concluded that a garden that cost $300 to start could not begin to pay for itself until the third year. But thereafter, he calculated, assuming at least a ten-year life expectancy for the shovel, spade, hoe, rake, wheelbarrow, trowel, and garden hose, and allowing for the probable increase in the costs of seeds, water rates, and fertilizers, the garden certainly would pay off — providing he did not add in the cost of his labor. On the other hand, it would really pay off if he called slavery "recreation" and credited himself for the hours spent in the garden with the money he would have spent on amusements for the same number of hours. So he talked about money as he spaded his garden, but what he was really talking about was having fun.

Other people were having fun, too, even if things sometimes went wrong. The *New York Times* discovered a schoolteacher in Atlanta, Georgia, who told them, "Well, I don't know what happened.

"First we had the blossom-end rot on the tomatoes and lost some," she said, "but there were a lot left, so I called the county agent and she gave me instructions on how to can them, so I did four quarts. They spoiled. Then I froze some okra and tomatoes, and they exploded. Boom. I think it was because I let the cat into the garden. The garden god was after me. But the lettuce was wonderful, and I'm going to do it again."

A woman in Little Rock, Arkansas, also gardening for the first time in her life, made the mistake of not knowing how heavily tomato plants bear — and thus not knowing how many plants to set out. She shortly discovered that ripe tomatoes were not only taking up all the shelves in her pantry, but were also filling her guest bed and all the bureau drawers in the guest bedroom, and even while she frantically made gallons of catsup, more tomatoes were ripening in the garden. Her next-door neighbor was meanwhile busily watering, planting, fertilizing, mulching, weeding, and praying over tomatoes, squash, herbs, cucumbers, marigolds, sunflowers, eggplants, peppers, green beans, snow peas, and asparagus. But the herbs failed to grow, and the marigolds sickened. Then something ate the tomatoes, peppers, and eggplants, and everything else died except two squash, four cucumbers, one marigold, and one dinner's worth of beans. Another tyro set out so much basil that he wound up with three grocery bags full.

But such disasters and misjudgments were almost as enjoyable to the novice gardeners as success would have been. They loved to talk and laugh about their errors, and promised to return to their gardens next year with the lessons of experience well in mind. I believe the fundamental reason for keeping a garden, be it only a windowbox of herbs, has to do with a desire to be creative; to do things just a bit differently; to enjoy a feeling of accomplishment. In this context, the fact that a garden can produce good food is of high, but secondary, importance. Speaking as one who kept a garden and a flock of chickens when we had a country place, I can testify to the time and effort this required, and to the taste of food fresh from the garden, and the taste of fertile eggs and of decently raised birds. But important as the delights of the table were, of greater importance was the satisfaction of having done something by and for oneself. And here, I think, is the real reason for the sudden, nationwide enthusiasm for gardening that erupted in 1974. I think the high food prices of that year were more important subconsciously than they were overtly — because, broadly speaking, it was not the poor who turned to gardening, but the reasonably affluent middle class. I think the high store prices served to remind people of something of which they had for a long time been subconsciously aware: the food in the stores was not as good as food could be; the store food was the product of a system that ought to work better than it does; there was something people could do that would at once express their defiance of the system and give them a feeling of self-sufficient independence and real personal accomplishment. I think the year of Watergate led people to Candide's conclusion that the thing to do was to cultivate our garden.

In this presumption, I have the support of at least one psychiatrist, who is fond of saying that when one is confronted by an enemy or a problem, one has three choices: to surrender, to fight, or to run. By this measurement, the escapers and gardeners we have been considering could be regarded as those who are trying to do what they can to win free. But some of them also join with others in taking a fierce joy in direct, hand-to-hand combat with the system.

The counterattackers are determined not to let the stores push them around. They know to the mill the price of every foodstuff in every supermarket available to them. They clip all the cents-off coupons from magazines and newspapers. They shop for specials. They go to one store for meat and to another for produce, changing stores as the prices vary. They read all the food advertisements word for word, minutely inspect the labels on the packages, and buy the house brands that shelter under the nationally advertised standard brands. The house brand is a product made by a subsidiary firm of the supermarket that sells it. It will be as good, if not better, than the nationally advertised one, but it will cost less. One reason why the house brand can be sold for less is that no money is spent to advertise it: the supermarket in effect lets the national brand people spend the money to bait the customer into the store where, next to the advertised brand, he finds the cheaper house brand on the same shelf.

The counterattackers include crusaders who enter the supermarkets with suspicion tempered by disgust — and hope. It is as if they will be crushed if they cannot find a rancid steak or a dud bird in order to be able to report this to the local representative of the U.S. Department of Agriculture. They have the names and addresses of all the federal, city, and state agencies at memory's fingertips. False or misleading advertising is to be reported to the Federal Trade Commission, the crusaders will tell you. Mislabeled, insanitary, or spoiled food, other than meat and poultry, should be reported to the Federal Drug Administration. If they spy a fly in a store, they call the local health department. If they see household products and toys they believe to be hazardous to children, they are at once on the telephone to the Consumer Product Safety Commission. They are the same people who call the U.S. Postal Service whenever they receive unsolicited products by mail, and who alert the Environmental Protection Agency whenever they believe they have discovered someone polluting the air or water. Organized into self-appointed consumer protection groups, the crusaders are the necessary shock troops of the armies of reform. Sometimes it is difficult to judge whether their interest in befriending the consumer is greater than their interest in going to war with a corporation, but no matter. They see the system as working badly, they would reform it if they can, and they meanwhile claw back at it.

Some of the crusaders see the enemy as ourselves, and one of them is a woman who wants to enlist everyone in her movement, called SOS, or Stay Out of Stores. Signing herself Mrs. R., she advised readers of a newspaper's food pages to "make a list and do a full week's grocery shopping at one time. Plan paper bag lunches. Fill the car with gas if it has to be used. Then stay out of stores for a week.

"There is NO purchase," she wrote, "that can't be postponed for one week, and the result is that many 'wants' have disappeared in the meanwhile. You still have the cash in the bank, or in one of those budget envelopes. Mark them SOS Profits. Really, it works. SOS also works on a selected basis

for longer periods. Buy no clothing for a month. The delay
forces you to plan ahead and thereby get better buys without
impulse spending. Or buy no games, books, or toys for a
month. Instead, get out the old ones or teach the kids a
couple of new card games.''

However cogent Mrs. R.'s advice might seem, it has all the
emotional ring of the Repentant Consumer coming down the
sawdust trail and up to the altar to bear witness that she's
now seen the Light. Starting out with food, she wound up
talking about everything else, and one gathers it is not really
money she wants to save. She wants to save us all from
ourselves. She wants to wean us from the impulsive consumption she sees as a kind of harmful national addiction.
She wants us to live differently from the way she thinks we
do, and this is a point that all the various escapers, gardeners,
prudent shoppers, and crusaders share.

It is also the point made by those who prefer to fly rather
than to fight. Their number particularly includes a good
many young people who believe there is no alternative but to
step outside the system altogether. Here, it must be said that
the search for an alternative is predominantly a middle-class
enthusiasm. The rich seem to be perfectly satisfied with the
way things are, but they live above the battle. There is not
much the poor can do to change their circumstances, for it is
all they can do to endure them. But the middle class has the
motive, the means, and the opportunity to live differently
from the way they do, and a great many members of the
middle class who are desirous of change would entirely
understand the Harvard lad who dropped out of college to
take up carpentry — arguing that "I want to get back to
basics."

It seems to me that getting back to basics is the rationale of
the young people who, in increasing numbers, are joining
farm communes. They, like the young man who extolled the

virtues of his macrobiotic diet, are concerned about spiritual salvation, which they believe to be based on living understandingly together in harmony with nature. This might seem to be a radical regression to social infancy, to the first tribal village to appear at the dawn of the age of agriculture. But it might also be seen as a search for independence as well as a search for religious experience.

Getting back to basics is also a primary reason why young people in the last two years have suddenly overcrowded the nation's agricultural colleges, at the very time other college enrollment was dropping so drastically as to threaten universities with economic disaster.

A search for escape from a way of life that seems unreal, or so unduly complicated as to be unrealistic, is by no means confined to the young. It is sufficiently widespread to have recalled into print *Five Acres and Independence: A Handbook for Small Farm Management* by M. G. Kains. The book first appeared at the very nadir of the Great Depression of the 1930s. Its reappearance during the depression of the 1970s was purely coincidental, unless one should take the view that economic disappointments call other disappointments to mind. The basic message of the book has nothing to do with economics. It is a diatribe against urban life, a literary banzai charge against the wicked cities of the plain.

The city dweller, Mr. Kains says, is a cliff dweller who does not know or want to know others housed under the same roof:

> His children "have no place to go but out and no place to come but in . . . He and they are eking out a narrowing, uneducative, imitative, more or less selfish and purposeless existence . . . His and their "expectation of life" is shortened by tainted air, restricted sunshine, and lack of exercise, to say nothing of exposure to disease.

Contrasted with all these and other city existence characteristics are the permanence and productivity of land, whether only a small suburban lot or a whole farm; the self-reliance of the man himself and that developed in each member of his family; the responsibility and satisfaction of home ownership against leasehold; the health and happiness typical not only of the life itself but of the wholesome association with genuine neighbors who reciprocate in kind and degree as few city dwellers know how to do; the probably longer and more enjoyable "expectation of life" but, best of all, the basis and superstructure of true success — development and revelation of character and citizenship in himself, his wife, sons and daughters.

Which, think you, is the better citizen, the man who pays rent for a hall room, a hotel suite or a "flat," or the one who owns a self-supporting rural home and therein rears a family of sons and daughters by the labors of his head and his hands and their assistance.

In a poignant sense city existence is non-productive; it deals with what has been produced elsewhere. Moreover, it is dependent upon "income" to supply "outgo" and in the majority of cases has nothing to show, not even character, for all the time and money spent.

Before we all shout Amen! we might recall that rural life can, in a poignant sense, be nonproductive, too. Almost by definition, civilization occurs only in cities. A possible exception might be a society exclusively composed of gentlemen farmers, all of whom were as well educated, multifariously talented, and endlessly inventive as Thomas Jefferson. Unfortunately, there are no such societies, and the chances are remote that there ever will be. What a rural society most usually produces, in addition to turnips, children, and blisters, is a strong but limited character and an exceedingly narrow life of the mind. One logical and living example of what the young communal farmers and Mr. Kains advocate is the Pennsylvania Dutch community.

The people are descendants of Germans who have preserved their way of life intact for more than two hundred
years. They decided to drop out from the eighteenth century,
and as a consequence, have had nothing to do with the
nineteenth and twentieth centuries, either. Their lives are
lived within the terms of a religion that forbids gauds and
fripperies, and that binds them to the soil in perpetual
obedience to God's command to Adam. The Plain People
are, in a word, farmers.

They all wear somber and old-fashioned clothing: the girls
and women in bonnets and long-sleeved, full-skirted dresses;
the boys and men in black trousers, black coats, and round,
low-crowned black hats. Thus attired, they drive through
their fertile and immaculately manicured countryside in
black buggies. They have no more use for modern farm
machinery than they have for automobiles, and not simply
because "tractors don't give manure," as one of them said.
Their opposition to modernity is deliberate, steadfast, and
religious. The Plain People either know or fear that to give
an inch to modernity would inevitably result in a loss of faith
and in the consequent loss of a way of life consistent with
that faith.

While not all of us might want to embrace either their faith
or their ways, we can certainly be impressed by the results of
their husbandry. The same families have operated general
farms on the same land since their ancestors cleared the
wilderness, and they have been consistently prosperous ever
since, working that land by hand labor and horsepower. If
anyone says the general family farm is not an economically
viable proposition in America today, the Plain People stand
ready to refute him. They are the living proof that the family
farm can be more efficient in terms of cost and yield than a
corporate farm. More than self-sufficient, the Plain People
bring a famous surplus to market. Their diet is varied and

ample; they sit to tables featuring the seven sweets and seven sours of their nourishing and distinctive cuisine.

The Plain People have survived because they are a like-minded community devoutly adherent to a religious discipline, *and* because all the rest of us have allowed them to live among us without demanding that they serve in our armies and engage in other duties of citizenship that we must carry out. The Plain People are independent only in the sense that they have nothing to do with the outside world except sell their surplus to the specialty markets that feature Pennsylvania Dutch foodstuffs. In all other senses of the word, they are not at all independent. They are held within traditions and a discipline that claim their minds and condition all their responses. They have chosen to remain at a particular point in social development. It is extremely doubtful that one family of Plain People could survive alone in the modern world. They can, however, survive in their own little theocracy, with our permission.

I suggest that their Weltanschauung is infinitely more emotional than it is rational, and that this must be the case with anyone who wants to take to the woods and fields and let the world go rot while he cultivates his garden. The Plain People certainly prove that you can do this, provided you know what you are doing and are willing and able to work like a German. You can do this on five acres, as Mr. Kains says, and millions of people elsewhere in the world are making a living on much less land than that. Of course you can keep your expenses low by buying nothing, providing you live within a society of like minds and trade by barter. The impulse to live a simple, pacifistic communal life is an extremely powerful one, always present in each of us, and emergent in times of stress. It was no doubt responsible for the popularity of monasteries during an earlier Dark Age. But a trouble with monasteries and other rural theocracies is that they are precisely as mobile and as visionary as so many ostriches with their heads in sand.

On the other hand, the Plain People are alive and well in Pennsylvania, and quite well fed. We might think their society is going nowhere, but they think they are going to Heaven by the only available route. This going to Heaven is also the rationale of the young communal farmers. Their arguments, as I understand them, seem to include the notion that what one does on earth is really of no matter when seen from the aspect of eternity. You can become president of General Motors, if that sort of thing amuses you, or Joan of Arc, or Queen Marie of Rumania. Human life has no objective meaning. Therefore, if you are disappointed by the way of life you know, why not embrace another way? Why not return to the land, and let the cities drown in their own slime? Why not create Heaven on earth by establishing a communal Peaceable Kingdom during the only life we know?

Such arguments are not entirely without merit, but if anyone wants to become a latter-day pioneer, I have a word of advice for him: Take money. A modest fortune may not be quite enough. Bear in mind that the accountant figured the start-up cost of his backyard garden at more than $300. The acquisition and start-up costs of a five-acre farm on good land can easily run beyond $100,000. It seems reasonable to believe that anyone nowadays who wishes to acquire five acres and independence had better be independently wealthy before he begins.

To drop out and go back to the land is certainly one of the middle-class options. A small number of people are taking it up. The importance of this movement, however, is that these people are not simply running away; they are, instead, running *toward* something they believe will be better.

And this, I think, is what all the various dissenters,

crusaders, and intelligent escapers are doing and saying in their different ways. People who try to create something of a family life in a society that is organized in a pattern inimical to family life; people who express a concern for the table; people who garden and otherwise seek out ways to avoid supermarket fare and pass by McDonald stands without a glance — all these people are not just so many malcontents saying no to a society that most people accept. They are saying yes to something. They are saying yes to life.

The more general the dissatisfaction becomes, the greater the possibility of change. The food industry's grip on the public throat is not unbreakable. The industry and the supermarkets are respectful of public demand. They spend fortunes in advertising dollars trying to create such demand. If people generally stopped buying what they now sell, they would offer what was wanted; the industry after all wants to make money, and if the society should change then so would the industry. I do not believe that much will change tomorrow or even next week; my point is merely that the level of dissatisfaction is directly related to the possibility of change, and that good can come from dissent. It is meanwhile interesting and a reason for hope to find so many dissenters engaged in a positive search for gastronomic life, liberty, and happiness in modern America.

A Thought for Food

Perhaps you will have noticed an underlying and unifying theme in all that has been said so far. In almost all the conversations and interviews recorded for this book, the controlling word was "feel," not "food." Even the New Food engineers talked about "mouthfeel." When we talk about food, we tend to talk about cost, nutrition, and taste.

But eating is one of the most personal things we do, and whenever we talk about food, the emotions are engaged. The words "fight," "accept," "escape," and "dissent" all carry an emotional freight. What we feel about food we also feel about the system that produces it; if anyone says that he does not like American food, he is also saying that there is something about America he does not like, and the reverse is just as true. It is feeling that gives rise to thought, and thought to action; the Renaissance was nothing if not an emotional experience. I have suggested there is a ferment that could lead to an American gastronomic renaissance, and I believe this ferment is, at heart, an emotional one. All the critics of the food industry whose words I have read have spoken with the accents of Jeremiah, and I would suppose this is because they have all dealt with a matter that lies, so to speak, at the pit of our stomachs. But since none of the critical writings has dealt directly with the importance of the emotions, I propose that we break new ground and do so — beginning with the emotions of the person who most usually buys the family food and puts it on the table.

Generally speaking, that person is Mom. She knows that she is supposed to buy good things of sound value at the lowest possible price. She has been advised to cook adventurously and see to it that every adventure has a happy ending. Then, as if this were not enough of a burden to lug home from the store and put on the stove, she is further supposed to be the creator of the happy home — just as if one person could possibly create such a thing all by herself and as if that one person were always dear old Mom, ever ready to assuage everyone's hurt feelings with her wonderful home cooking. That, I think, is the final straw, landing on Mommy's back with the impact of an office safe falling fourteen stories.

"Shopping is a very, very difficult thing," one woman assured me, "and the woman gets very little thanks for it.

When you go into a supermarket, there you are, all by
yourself, out there in the jungle. You are assaulted by giant
quarts and jumbo pounds. I guess they don't do that
anymore, but you know what I mean. If they can't get you
one way, they try to get you in another. Believe me, it's a
jungle. And you have to plan what you are going to eat,
three hundred and sixty-five days a year, and nobody really
gives you credit for this, any more than people notice the
plaster on the wall until it cracks and falls down, and then
they say, 'Oh, look, your plaster's falling; you'll have to fix it.'

"You're supposed," she said, "to be imaginative and
inventive, but it is certainly not easy to be imaginative every
day in the year, and particularly when, every time you go
into the store, you see the same old things in the same old
places, looking just the same as the last time you saw them
— and certainly you can't feel creative if you're pushed for
time and have to buy something and get out of there because
you have so much else to do. You're not supposed to let
yourself be cheated by the beasts in the jungle, and if you
have to worry about not remembering to bring the coupon to
get ten cents off the cake mix, or worry that you just paid
three cents more for carrots at Giant than you would have
paid at Safeway, why, then if there ever was any fun in
shopping, those things just take all the fun out of it.

"What I mean to say is that everybody just takes it for
granted that you go to the store and buy the food, and
nobody ever compliments you for doing this. When my
daughter complained about what there was to eat one night,
I fixed her. I told her if she didn't like what I cooked, she
could go to the store next day — I wasn't going to go — and
she could cook dinner the next night. Well, next day she
dragged her feet and dragged her feet until, at the last
minute, just before the store closed at six, she went to the
store and you know what she bought? Hamburger! She saw

all those meats in the case and she didn't know one from another or what to buy or how much to ask for or what she ought to pay for it or how to cook it, so she took the easy way out and came home with this lump of gray hamburger and *that* was the big improvement! After that, she never had another word to say about my shopping. She found out it wasn't all that easy."

The woman spoke about this quite calmly, unaware that she was setting forth a formidable catalogue of emotions. These included fear, loneliness, a feeling that no one appreciated her, frustration, and a desire for revenge upon her daughter. All this was embedded in what was ostensibly a statement about the difficulties of shopping.

So powerful is the emotional context within which food is gathered, cooked, and eaten that simply to enter a store is to engage the emotions. The very look of the place will give the shopper some sort of feeling about it. If it seems a friendly place, the shopper feels confident; if it seems impersonal, the shopper may feel suspicious; if it is gigantic, the customer might feel herself denigrated. Four young wives, interviewed together, felt so strongly about the three supermarkets they patronized that they began to argue among themselves. Three of them thought that one of the supermarkets was dirty and said they never shopped there for that reason; the fourth, who did all of her shopping at that store, said it was not dirty at all and that the other stores were awful and overpriced. A rather bitter and nearly tearful quarrel ensued. Insofar as I could determine by subsequent inspection, all three supermarkets were remarkably alike with respect to merchandise, foodstuffs, prices, and cleanliness — but since I did not shop in any of them, and because my interest in them was purely clinical, I had no feelings about them one way or another. If I lived in that neighborhood and shopped in one of those stores, I would very likely have chosen to shop in it for some emotional reason, because there were no apparent rational reasons for making a choice.

Speaking of choice, any negative feelings we may have about shopping for food are certainly exacerbated whenever we discover that the choice offered us in supermarkets is more apparent than real. Several yards of shelves, four-tiers high, will be gaudy with all manner of shapes and sizes and brands of canned and bottled tomato sauce, all at different prices. Along these yards of shelf space, the store is not selling different things; it is selling the same thing. Every bit of it is tomato sauce, and for all the difference in sizes, prices, and brand names, the taste of any one of those tomato sauces is strikingly similar to the taste of any other, and so is the nutrient value. The same point can be made with respect to shelves full of seemingly, but not actually, very different cookies, detergents, cake mixes, soft drinks, breakfast cereals, and, indeed, almost any other products on the supermarket shelves.

This denial of real choice is all the more annoying because choice is diminishing at the very time that the public's concern for culinary affairs is becoming more sophisticated and demanding. The public trend became evident in the first postwar decades of mass aerial tourism to Europe. It is not snobbish or fashionable to say that European food is better than our own; it is simply to state a fact. The reasons for this are that the Europeans shop each day; that the bread is fresh-baked each day and all the other foods are farm-fresh that day; that all the fruits and produce are in season; that the Europeans give a great deal of their time and attention to food (a matter that helps to account for what we think is their different way and slower pace of life), and constitute, in sum, a demanding clientele that is knowledgeable in the kitchen. Whether the postwar tourist multitudes were aware of these matters, they at any rate returned to America with a knowledge that dinner could consist of something other than meat, potatoes, and a store-bought apple pie. Coincident with this tourism, and with the unprecedented prosperity that made the tourism possible, Irma Rombauer's *The Joy of Cooking* became the nation's standard cookbook. It had a European frame of reference to an extent that earlier favorites, such as *The Good Housekeeping Cookbook*, did not. Following closely upon Mrs. Rombauer's apron strings came all manner of exotic cookbooks that sold remarkably well. All through the postwar decades the food pages of the nation's magazines and metropolitan newspapers spoke with foreign accents, and Americans began to select and cook rather more adventurously than at any time in their past.

But also at this time the cities were losing their hinterland, the corporate farms were diminishing choice, the processing industry was growing apace, and the supermarkets were proliferating. By no means out of touch with popular enthusiasms, the supermarkets took notice of the public's adventuresomeness, but catered to it in a manner all their own. They began to use the word "gourmet" as an adjective, installing counters of what they called "gourmet foods." Here, in the 1950s, one could find canned rattlesnake, offered as a cocktail snack. There was, for a while, a rather more limited business done in chocolate-covered ants from Japan. And instead of carrying on their shelves the fresh ingredients from which one could make an Italian salad dressing, a Swiss fondue, or Mexican tamales, the supermarkets sold commercially prepared salad dressing and heat-and-serve fondue and tamales, along with all other manner of trash that no gourmet would allow in his house, much less in his kitchen.

The nineteen fifties and sixties were fad-prone decades, with the fads being the result, if not the creation, of the mass communications media's reporting, and thus we had fads in cookery just as in fashion and very nearly all else. One year onion soup was in, next year it was out; now it is lasagna, last

year it was chicken Kiev, and before that it was quiche
Lorraine. Prepared varieties of these foods appeared on the
gourmet or convenience food shelves of the supermarkets as
inevitably as night follows day. By the time America's baked
potatoes were drowning from coast to coast in an arctic
sludge of sour cream with chives in it (chopped frozen chives
were now available at your friendly neighborhood supermarket at a price only several thousand percent more than
fresh chives might have cost), Julia Child began to teach on
television. Dancing in from the wings, blithely sipping wine
as he chattered, came the Galloping Gourmet. The wild
success of these programs was an obvious demonstration of
an increasing national interest in cookery. Another program
followed: it was a series on Italian cookery, by the family
Romagnoli. It was almost as popular and, if put into
practice by the viewer, considerably less fattening than the
others.

This national interest in cookery is all to the good, being a
harbinger of the potential culinary renaissance in America I
have envisioned. But whether the renaissance will be a still
birth remains to be seen. It is one thing to learn how good
food can be and to learn by reading or by watching television
how to confect something quite delicious, and it is another
thing altogether to then go to the supermarket and discover
that the store does not carry the ingredients. How often have
you seen leeks in your friendly neighborhood supermarket?
If yours carries them, you are fortunate; mine does not. It is
frustrating not to be able to obtain what you need. It is
irritating to be offered inferior substitutes at ridiculous
prices, as in the case of frozen chives as a substitute for fresh
ones, or canned mushrooms for fresh ones. It is insulting to
be offered a precooked commercial product in lieu of the
ingredients you seek. Frustration, annoyance, and insult give
rise to a reasonably ugly emotion.

Together with a growing concern for difference in the

kitchen came a steadily increasing interest in nutrition. Alarms were being sounded throughout the land, warning everyone that the food industry was busily lacing its products with poisons, and with colors and chemicals that might prove to be poisonous. Other alarms warned us that, if what we ate was not poisoned, we must be sure not to poison ourselves through an inappropriate diet. Ah, well. Nutritional fads have long been with us. My own generation was raised on spinach. Once we were all told to warm the baby's bottle. Now we are told you can give the little fellow ice cream if you wish, because the temperature of the milk is unimportant. Once we were told to give children lots of milk. Now we are told that milk can be bad for them because it has so much sodium in it. The daily egg of yesteryear has now become the daily dollop of cholesterol productive of an early grave. Insufficient roughage can result in cancer of the bowel, we hear. Do not breathe in; the air is poisoned. Don't go near the water; it is polluted. If you take an aspirin tablet for your headache, it will make a hole in your stomach. Don't take a bite of that apple, Eve! You have to wash it first. The next thing we might expect to hear would be the voice of the Surgeon General, solemnly warning us that eating is hazardous to our health. Heaven only knows what tomorrow's food fads and medical advice will be. It ought to be comforting to reflect that Eskimos do well on whale blubber; that Masai warriors prosper on the blood of their cattle; that Mongols largely subsist on mares' milk and yak butter; that one man's meat is another man's poison — and that today's science is tomorrow's rubbish.

But it is difficult for us to cling to such comforts, committed as we are to the idea that today's science is infallible; submitted as we are to a daily barrage of scientific warnings and advice; concerned as we are for the state of our family's health; and accustomed as we are to thinking that we ought to try whatever the advertisers tell us everyone else is buying and eating.

Here, for example, is a woman in a supermarket, trying to figure out the nutritive content of the foodstuffs, then comparing the prices so as to arrive at a maximum nutritional value at a minimum cost. I think it fair to say that we are in the presence of an emotional volcano approaching the point of eruption. We might at least be permitted the following deductions:

Her dominant emotion at the moment is one of profound suspicion. Therefore, unless she is so deranged as to take pleasure in suspicion, she is not having a rip-roaring good time.

Next, if she is so suspicious in her selection of foodstuffs, we may suppose her cookery to be more a matter of anxious chemistry than a happy work of unpremeditated art. If such a woman boils the wax beans an instant longer than she has been told she should, she will think she has boiled all the nourishment out of them, that her calculations have been wasted and her money lost, and that instead of nourishing her family she has just shot herself down in flames over her own stove. In any case, we might reasonably suppose that, if her shopping has a grim and wary aspect, her cookery will have its moments of quiet desperation.

This will be particularly true if she is caught up in the national enthusiasm for the different, but then attempts to prepare the popular difference of the moment. In such a case, her cookery will not be creative, but imitative and competitive, and just a bit more anxious than need be.

Let us further suppose that our suspicious shopper and anxious cook is the officer in charge of feeding the troops. Napoleon has assured her that her little army, like his own and any other, marches on its stomach. But the food that she puts on the table is not always the determining factor with respect to the family's morale. Napoleon's advice does not apply to defeated armies.

For instance, if a boy comes to the table and says he is too tired to eat, he does not necessarily mean he thinks Mom's food is terrible or that he is actually exhausted after his tough day at school. What he may have in mind is his passing dislike for his sister or for everyone else at the table, and wishes to be excused. Someone else, eating with good appetite, can be put off his feed by something someone says. If the father loudly announces his loathing for eggplant, this may be because he had to finish everything on his plate as a child and eggplant was a staple in his family's diet, and so whenever he sees an eggplant he subconsciously associates it with a gustatorially disastrous childhood. Or he may be using the eggplant as a club with which to belabor his wife for reasons quite unknown to her and, possibly, to himself. The table can be a silent, stricken field as easily as it can be the well-loved center of a loving family life. Children are particularly quick at sensing their parents' moods, especially that of their mother. You are not eating, a mother might say, and there is no way the children, sitting around a strangely ominous table, can demand to know what is wrong between Mom and Dad.

The table can also be a place of subterfuge and deceit. No less than one third of our respondents said they did not enjoy eating as a child, and one of them remembered diverting her parents' attention in order to cram the last bite of the detested asparagus down into her shoe. In two of every three families we questioned, there was at least one picky eater, almost always a male, who would refuse to eat a certain food for reasons that had nothing to do with its taste or value. In one of every four families we know, there is someone who is allergic to a certain food, and there is reason to believe in these cases that the allergy is a psychosomatic one, family connected.

None of this has to do with either the food or the cookery. Food does not determine appetite. The French are aware of this. When they wish you *bon appétit,* they are not expressing the hope that you are famished; they are wishing you joy of what ought to be a pleasant occasion. However delicious it might be, the food on the family dinner table, like the wafer and the wine, is by no means so important as the communion of which it is the symbol. If there is something wrong with the communion, there is probably more wrong with the family than with the food, and what is wrong with the family might very well be something that only a change in their way of life might cure. As we have seen, the evening meal is the modern urban American family's principal opportunity to hold communion, and it is not so much that the meal is the source of their morale, as that the family members each bring to the occasion whatever morale they have acquired during the day, and these emotions are served up along with the food.

If a woman believes that the food she serves makes the difference between a happy and an unhappy home, she is very much mistaken — or grossly misinformed. Good food can make a happy home happier, but that is all one can say. I have known families to be miserable even when the table was glorious with a standing rib roast of prime beef.

Given the emotional context in which food is procured, prepared, and eaten, it would seem to be sensible to avoid or alleviate the destructive emotions, and give free play to the constructive ones. Just how anyone wishes to go about this is his business, not yours or mine, but I would suggest that the first thing anyone could do would be to relax.

For instance, it does your digestion no good to rage against store bread, when the obvious answer is to bake your own. Whole wheat, rye, unbleached, and many other flours are available in a great many supermarkets, along with those loaves apparently made of Dacron and nylon. The process is simplicity itself. You mix and knead the dough in a few minutes, and put it aside to rise while you go about your other lawful occasions. Later you put the risen dough into bread pans and pop them into the oven and forget about them until they are done. Where is all the time and effort of which people complain?

Nor does it do any good to stew over the fact that you cannot prepare a dish that Julia Child makes because you cannot find in your store the ingredients she can find in hers. Indeed, many of the ingredients of French and Italian cookery are found nowhere other than in France and Italy, and then only in particular regions of those countries. No purpose is served by using substitutes. Nor is any purpose served by attempting the dish of the moment because other people are doing so. The relaxed view of the matter would seem to entail remembering that any renaissance is based upon suggestion and invention, not upon prescription, and remembering· that the art of cookery, like any other art, is much more personal than competitive. The good thing about America's increased interest in sophisticated cuisine is the possibility that this interest will lead to experimentation and thus to the personal satisfaction of the creative impulse. More than one housewife watches the cooking shows and reads cookbooks for what ideas they suggest; these women do not regard the information as a list of immutable instructions. I would say such cooks are wise.

It is true that much that is sold from supermarket shelves is an insult to the ordinary intelligence, but why rage against those preposterous dry breakfast cereals when the sensible thing to do is ignore them? Oh, to be sure you see them on the shelves, much as you might notice a dog's mess on the pavement, but the thing to do, I think, is to recognize the mess and avoid it and immediately forget it.

Similarly, one might choose to ignore all the packaged and convenience foods. Let those who will eat them: I know we are enjoined to be our brother's keeper, but sometimes I wonder where is the best place to keep him, and at other times I think there are more than enough people in the world as it is. To put the matter more positively, it seems important to me to fight the right battle at the right place at the right time with the right weapons, and the time and place to fight against the indecencies of the food processors is not when you are in the store looking for something to eat for dinner.

Limited as the supermarket's offerings may be, and stale or treated as some of its fruits and produce may be, not every foodstuff will be wholly bad. I would certainly agree that the overall effect of the supermarket is disappointing and that the entire concept of supermarket operation deserves all the contempt we can muster — and remedial legislation. But the time to hate the store is not at the moment of shopping, when the simple idea is to get out of the place with something nourishing and tasty at a price we can manage. Granted that frozen food is not quite as nourishing or as tasty as its fresh equivalent; still it is by no means devoid of taste and nutritional value, and on any given day, the frozen broccoli might be a much better buy than the cheap, yellowing, ratty broccoli in the fresh produce bin. Why not take a chance that the frozen broccoli has not been thawed and refrozen half a dozen times, through slipshod handling and general mismanagement, before you take it from the case? It will certainly be better than what you see decaying in the bin, and you can always hope for better luck tomorrow.

If there is an available alternative to the supermarket, and if supermarkets disgust you, then the thing to do is stay out of supermarkets.

In saying these things, I merely suggest that, since shopping for food is an emotional experience, the thing to do while you are in the store would seem to be to get what you can, accept what you must, and leave.

Nor should a concern for nutrition cause the shopper to pound around the aisles, livid with fury. No one needs a balanced meal every day. In fact, no one needs to eat every day. It is quite enough to balance the diet of a week or even a month. The fresh meats, fish, poultry, fruit, leafy vegetables, root vegetables, and dairy products sold in the supermarkets have not been drenched with poisons by genocidal corporations — at least not to the extent some of the alarmists would have us believe — and they have certainly not been treated with the pharmacopoeia employed in the preparation and packaging of processed foods. Anyone whose diet includes a portion of each of these fresh foods, together with whole grain, will receive all the nutrients he needs. Where fresh fruits and vegetables are lacking, then their frozen equivalents are the next best thing. Anyone who passes by all those bottles, cans, and packages on the shelves, and repairs instead to the fresh food counters, need not worry about nutrition or try to make sense out of all those labels.

When we consider nutrition, we might have a thought for the people of Tuscany, who enjoy one of the world's most healthful diets and most distinguished cuisines. Centuries ago it was the Tuscans who invented the fork and taught the French how to cook. I know, from having kept house in Tuscany for two years, that the people employ olive or other vegetable oil in their cookery instead of butter or animal fats. Salt and sugar are virtually absent from their foods, as compared with our own. Lean veal, not fat beef, appears on Tuscan tables, along with rabbit, chicken, seafood, and game in season. Since meat and seafood are quite expensive, the Tuscans buy sparingly of these foods — although there is perhaps another reason. At one point Caesar reports his troops complaining that they had to eat beef in Gaul when the supply of flour fell short. Meat seems never to have loomed so large in the Italian diet as it does in our own. However this may be, the Tuscan diet is lavish with fresh vegetables, leafy greens, and fruit, and partly because of their healthful diet, and partly because of the great amount of exercise Tuscans take in walking about the steep stone streets of their hill towns, the people carry far less average tonnage on them than Americans do — despite the daily Italian ingestion of pasta.

They are a remarkably lean, handsome, and healthy people who are in love with eating and whose joy it is to eat foods in season. Their diet of seasonal foods owes nothing to the fact that most Tuscans lack the refrigerators and freeze lockers of the Americans. It has everything to do with taste and anticipated pleasure. They are content to wait for the Sicilian blood oranges, for example, and to relish them while they last, rather than to buy oranges from somewhere else all year long, much less frozen orange juice. So too might rural Americans be content to wait till their own asparagus, peas, corn, or apples are ripe, and refuse to eat any other at any other time of year. This attitude is essentially one of celebration; every season brings its own thanksgiving; the parade of seasonal foodstuffs marks the turning year. In Italy, the appearance of the ripe figs is cause for rejoicing. The Italian day is built around the noon meal, and this is not the worker's lunch at a cafeteria or the businessman's lunch at a restaurant; it is enjoyed at home by the entire family — which, unlike the American family, is an extensive one. The children come home from school, the parents from their work, and from noon till four Italy is at table at home, and then is taking its siesta. There is also a strong quality of religious life in Tuscany, and by this I do not refer to the Catholic faith, although that is indeed important and is in part celebrated by the appearance of special foods prepared only on various saints' days. I refer to the older gods, the lares and penates, those of the household, whose presence may be more keenly felt by a foreigner like myself than by the Italian families.

You will have noticed a religious cast throughout this discussion, for it is my belief that a mystery lies at the center of the emotional context within which food is gathered, prepared, and eaten. All those people out there in modern Ohio, praying over their soybeans, have something in common with the Nilotic culture of the First Kingdom, and with the woman who suspected the garden god was after her, and with the one who prayed as she mulched. All are celebrants of a mystery. I know of no religion that did or does not pay its respects to food, praying for harvests, making use of food in its rituals, and/or like the Muslims, Catholics, and Jews, mysteriously establishing dietary laws that make no rational sense. The animists, pagans, and deists are as one in this matter. The various nations of American Indians spoke different languages, but in each of them, whatever the word they used for corn, that word meant the same thing: "Our Life." In their animistic religions, as in every other, food had its mystical importance. I can think of no religious festival that does not have its appropriate food. However little any one of us might care for organized religion, I believe that all of us are still responsive to a mystery that has held mankind's attention since the invention of agriculture. I believe none of us is immune to it, and that we need to delve in a bit of earth, even though it be in a flowerpot, wherein to sow and reap a harvest, and so enter into communion with all generations, past, present, and future. I daresay this mysterious need lay beneath whatever other reasons impelled unprecedented numbers of Americans to start gardening while food prices climbed, particularly inasmuch as we have seen that a concern for saving money had little or nothing to do with this phenomenon.

I believe that when we talk about food we are talking about life, and most usually we are talking about the holy trinity of man, woman, and child. We are what we eat; we eat what we are. So we receive our just desserts. When the price of food goes up, we are more keenly aware of this than we are of an increase in the price of automobiles, because food lies at the center of family life, whereas automobiles do not. Therefore we see in the rising price of food a threat to our family's life — even if we can afford the higher price. Similarly, if processors debase or distort food, and middlemen gouge, and supermarkets deceive, whatever we might rationally think of these practices is as nothing to what we subconsciously *feel* about them. We might talk about poisons and prices, but a reason why we talk so bitterly is our feeling that the temple has been profaned by the money-changers; that every distortion and deception is a sacrilegious mockery of the mystery of life and of the trinity. We subconsciously think, These people are out to kill us.

When we set out our gardens, when we make our conscientious selection of foodstuffs, when we go to work in our kitchens and dress our dinner tables, we are celebrants of an immemorial mystery, going through the appropriate rituals. The ultimate and principal ritual in our celebration is the evening communion around the dinner table. This is our daily statement of faith, our daily thanksgiving, and the way we celebrate it reveals what we believe to be true about ourselves. First and last there is the food itself, but more than food is involved. We express our view of the life we have by what we wear, by our manners, by our behavior to one another, by what we find to say, by our choice of the room in which our communion is held, by the art with which it is adorned, by how we serve the food, and by how long we remain at table — all of which is to say that the entire circumstances of the evening meal combine to state what family life means to us and what we actually think of one another.